# WHEN JESUS RETURNS

## JAN MARKELL

GENERAL EDITOR

**HARVEST PROPHECY**
AN IMPRINT OF HARVEST HOUSE PUBLISHERS

Cover design by Studio Gearbox

Cover images © Aleksandra Vinogradova, tomertu / Shutterstock

Interior design by KUHN Design Group

For bulk, special sales, or ministry purchases, please call 1-800-547-8979.
Email: CustomerService@hhpbooks.com

This logo is a federally registered trademark of the Hawkins Children's LLC. Harvest House Publishers, Inc., is the exclusive licensee of this trademark.

**When Jesus Returns**
Copyright © 2024 by Jan Markell
Published by Harvest House Publishers
Eugene, Oregon 97408
www.harvesthousepublishers.com

ISBN 978-0-7369-8960-2 (pbk)
ISBN 978-0-7369-8961-9 (eBook)

Library of Congress Control Number: 2024931181

**Printed in the United States of America**

24 25 26 27 28 29 30 31 32 / BP / 10 9 8 7 6 5 4 3 2 1

This book is dedicated to all sincere saints who have faithfully searched for a solid, Bible-believing church. Some of you are blessed to have found one, and others are still looking, traveling many miles weekly and getting discouraged. Don't give up!

As Hebrews 10:25 says, we must gather together to encourage one another—and all the more as we see the day approaching.

*That day is indeed drawing near!*

## ACKNOWLEDGMENTS

Olive Tree Ministries' 22 international conferences could not have transpired without our dedicated staff and volunteers. I am deeply thankful for them. Many turned up before dawn to finalize so many wonderful, life-changing events. And they showed up year after year, never daunted by the backbreaking work nor the thousands of people with so many needs. More will be in eternity thanks to this selfless enthusiasm!

# CONTENTS

# FOREWORD

AMIR TSARFATI

I n the final chapter of the Bible, Jesus said, "I am coming quickly." He said it not once, not twice, but three times (Revelation 22:7, 12, 20). There is no way to miss this promise. One time establishes a point, a second time drives it home, but the third time ensures that everyone sits up and takes notice. "Yes, what you've heard is true. I will be returning, and you better get ready because it won't be too long." If Jesus felt it was important for Him to give this promise a three-peat, then it should be important to us as well.

When the apostle Paul wrote about Christians as citizens of heaven, he put it this way: "Our citizenship is in heaven, from which we also *eagerly wait for the Savior*, the Lord Jesus Christ" (Philippians 3:20). According to Paul, to be a believer is also to eagerly anticipate the Lord's coming. The two go together.

During His last moments before the crucifixion, Jesus said to His disciples—and to us—"I will come again and receive you to Myself; that where I am, there you may be also" (John 14:3). As you read those words, can you sense His great affection for you, and how eager He is for you to be with Him?

In these ways and so many more, Jesus tells us that His return is a really big deal. Is it a big deal to us as well? It should be!

That's why I am grateful for the many Understanding the Times prophecy conferences Jan Markell has hosted over the years. I've had the privilege of teaching at several of these conferences. Every time I have done so, I've been incredibly blessed by the teachings and the opportunity to fellowship with dear brothers and sisters in Christ who are eager for His return.

Jan's love for Bible prophecy and her excited anticipation for our Lord's appearing is truly contagious. Because of her ministry, countless thousands of people around the world now have a great enthusiasm for Bible prophecy and live in eager expectancy of Christ's return.

*When Jesus Returns* brings together a wonderful collection of powerful messages spoken at Jan's prophecy conferences—messages that I know will instruct and encourage you deeply. You will come away more informed about God's plans for the future, and more excited about your place in those plans.

After Jesus repeated the promise of His return three times in Revelation 22, the apostle John was so excited he couldn't help but cry out, "Even so, come, Lord Jesus!" (verse 20).

My prayer is that by the time you finish reading *When Jesus Returns*, you'll find yourself eagerly echoing those very same words—all the way to the day of His glorious appearing!

—Amir Tsarfati

# OUR ASSIGNMENT TODAY

I began my radio career in 2001 in the Twin Cities with a program called *Understanding the Times*. It began as a live interview and call-in program. As a result of the program and format, I could easily get the pulse of those in my audience. And I concluded that they wanted to learn and to make sense of our times.

I also realized—again based on feedback—that most of our churches were silent on key issues. And the topic that underwhelmed them was Bible prophecy. *The pulpits were silent.* That is, they were silent about the fact that the stage-setting signs of Christ's return were on the increase and that planet Earth was running out of time. Jesus was going to return for His bride so very soon. Churches seemed to be embarrassed about this message!

So I decided I would start a conference ministry that would feature the best when it came to informing my audience about our times, and about the nearness of Christ's return in the clouds called the rapture. There are stage-setting signs exploding around us today, and someone has to sound the alarm: *We are running out of time.*

But at my first event in the spring of 2002, I never expected 1,500 people! And from there, enthusiasm and attendance only grew and grew as the Twin Cities became a destination for tens of thousands of people from around the world. Attendees would come from every state in America, every province in Canada, and a dozen foreign nations.

Imagine, people traveling—in some cases, thousands and thousands of miles—to learn, to fellowship, and to eagerly await His return together! Here, they found the like-minded. At such events they learned they could talk about their longing to hear the trumpet and a shout and not be mocked.

I am so thankful to Harvest House for allowing you and me to travel down memory lane and revisit some of the best messages given at a total of 22 conferences at various venues in Minneapolis-St. Paul. I do hope they help you be like the sons of Issachar, who understood the times (1 Chronicles 12:32).

I am convinced that is our assignment today!

CHAPTER 1

# HIDDEN IN PLAIN VIEW: THE NEW WORLD ORDER IN BIBLE PROPHECY

### JAN MARKELL

We hear a lot about the new world order. For those who aren't familiar with Bible prophecy, that term might not have much meaning. But biblically speaking, the new world order refers to the coming one-world government, over which the antichrist will rule. When we talk about the new world order, we're speaking of the antichrist's future kingdom. While that kingdom is not here yet, in a variety of ways, it has long been in the process of being built. Through the ages, Satan has made use of many tools to build this future kingdom, and eventually, the parts will come together as a global system.

On the surface, many of these tools don't necessarily appear to be part of Satan's agenda. But if we consider how these tools have steered the direction of humanity, we're able to see how they can contribute to the end result he desires to achieve. Just to name a few, Satan has used communism, socialism, and a wide variety of organizations, including the United Nations. International banking systems will eventually take us to a one-world economy. Issues like open borders and climate change are used to further globalism. The media and educational institutions help to advance ideas and concepts that emphasize man-centered global unity. And even supposedly Christian organizations can unwittingly contribute as vehicles that move us closer to a one-world system.

As of now, there are two huge obstacles that are making it difficult for Satan to bring his plans to fruition. One is the United States, which still has many who advocate national sovereignty and autonomy rather than globalism, and the other is Christianity, which affirms the biblical truth that it is impossible for sinful man to achieve the one-world utopia he so badly wants—only God can do that. That is why we are seeing both under attack as never before.

## THE PURSUIT OF A ONE-WORLD SYSTEM

Humanly speaking, man has always tried to achieve true and lasting peace and prosperity. Those are the goals that have long been touted by leaders, politicians, and governments. Mankind has also searched for relief from pain. But these pursuits have always been in vain and will continue to be. Yet they explain why there are people who are always looking for ways to make peace and prosperity happen. They set up programs and organizations in the hopes of reaching those goals. They want war and poverty and inequality to go away, but no matter what mankind tries to do, it fails. Satan has convinced people that if they only try harder, they will succeed. If only they can get everyone on board with the agenda, they can make things happen.

This is the kind of thinking that is behind all efforts made toward globalism, or a one-world system. But what many don't realize is they will never be successful because, at heart, mankind is evil. Only God can bring about the success man so desperately wants, because only He has the answer to mankind's problem of sin.

In recent decades in American politics, we have seen a growing number of clashes between nationalists and globalists. There are those who believe a country should function autonomously and make a priority of caring for the needs and concerns of its own people. And there are others who want America to submit to the globalist agenda.

We saw this happen during the 2016 presidential election, when Donald Trump ran against Hillary Clinton. In a campaign speech given in April 2016, Trump said, "We will no longer surrender this country or its people to the false song of globalism."[1] In contrast, Hillary's husband Bill, a former US president, founded the Clinton Global Initiative, which aims to create "a community of doers who are taking action on the world's most pressing challenges, together."[2]

This battle of agendas continues through today on many different fronts. And it's one of the reasons the globalist community is so critical of those who don't agree with them. In Israel, Benjamin Netanyahu has held to a nationalist position for the Jewish state, which has put him at odds with globalists. More recently, we've seen that with President Javier Milei of Argentina, whose policies run contrary to the globalist agenda.

At first glance, globalism seems innocent enough. We're told that it's all about cultures learning how to live together, appreciate one another, and make sacrifices for the common good. Globalist causes plead for people to give money and support that will make it possible to solve problems that will make the world a better place. What could possibly be wrong with that?

But in reality, globalism is about powerful leaders and organizations making decisions about how they believe the world should be run. They use their authority and resources to implement ideas and programs that supposedly are for the good of all, but ultimately, call for forced compliance or undermine human autonomy and freedom. And whether these power brokers know it or not, ultimately, they are paving the way for the future antichrist.

## THE HISTORY OF GLOBALISM

To give us some perspective on what's happening, I'd like to go back to where globalism first began—in ancient Babylon. The people who lived in the land of Shinar had become prideful and said, "Come, let us build ourselves a city, and a tower whose top is in the heavens; let us make a name for ourselves" (Genesis 11:4). This was an act of rebellion against God. And what did God do? He shut it down. He said, "This isn't a good idea." He then confused the people's languages, and they ended up being scattered around the world.

These same seeds of pride and destruction have been a part of every effort for a world order ever since. Ultimately, human pride rebels against God, and that leads to judgment.

## EUROPE'S PLACE IN
## THE PURSUIT OF GLOBALISM

You may be aware that in the middle of the sixteenth century, artist Pieter Bruegel painted what has since become one of his famous works, featuring the Tower of Babel. What's interesting is that this image—created nearly 500 years ago—was featured on a poster created by the European Community in the 1990s, which bore the slogan, "Europe: Many Tongues, One Voice." The poster announced the coming of the European Parliament building that now stands in Strasbourg, France—and the building bears an amazing resemblance to the Tower of Babel as depicted in Bruegel's painting.

So it seems as if there is a sense in which there are some who want to keep the idea of Babylon alive, even though it was an experiment that failed terribly.

A lot of what we are seeing happening today with Europe and the European Union will contribute to making it possible for the antichrist to rise to power. I agree with the Bible prophecy teachers who say that the antichrist will come out of Europe. In Daniel 9:26, we read that "the people of the prince who is to come shall destroy the city and the sanctuary." "The prince who is to come" is a reference to the future antichrist. And it is his predecessors—"the people" in the ancient Roman Empire—who came to Jerusalem to "destroy the city and the sanctuary" in AD 70.

Today, we see Europe facing many challenges. Europe is reeling from a variety of problems. A significant one is largely unchecked immigration, which has not worked out as planned. Huge numbers of Muslims from North Africa and the Middle East have moved to Europe but refused to integrate with European society. Other issues include political and economic disparities that have generated serious disagreements between the member nations of the European Union. The cover of the April 22, 2019 issue of *Time* magazine featured an article titled "The Unraveling of Europe." And a July 30, 2016 *Breitbart* article was headlined, "Polish Experts: 'Europe Is At the End of Its Existence. Western Europe Is Practically Dead.'"

I believe one of the biggest reasons for Europe's demise is its long-time rejection of God. When people throw God out of their lives, there are terrible consequences. And as long as Europe continues to decline, it's not hard to imagine there will come a day when everyone will be desperate enough to want a powerful leader who says he can set things right.

Among the current leaders of Europe are many globalists. They are active in the World Economic Forum and the European Union, and they have significant sway over what happens in European politics. They have significant influence over policies that affect all the member nations of the EU, and even the world. That's because other world governments who want to do business in Europe are expected to abide by policies established by the EU and are expected to abide by its rules. More and more, I believe we are seeing Europe move in a direction that will facilitate the rise of antichrist's global empire.

## THE BIBLICAL WARNINGS ABOUT
## THE FUTURE WORLD SYSTEM

In Revelation chapter 13, God reveals to us some important details about this coming one-world system. In connection with the beast, or the antichrist, we read this:

> He opened his mouth in blasphemy against God, to blaspheme His name, His tabernacle, and those who dwell in heaven. It was granted to him to make war with the saints and to overcome them. And authority was given him over every tribe, tongue, and nation. All who dwell on the earth will worship him (verses 6-8).

People all over the planet will worship the beast. He will have complete power over the entire globe. And he will persecute the saints—those who become Christians during the tribulation. All of this reveals to us the enormous extent of his power. He will oversee a truly global government and will war against those who aren't in agreement with him.

Daniel 11:36 gives us another glimpse of the antichrist's power: "The king shall do according to his own will; he shall exalt and magnify himself above every god, and shall speak blasphemies against the God of gods." In Revelation 17, we read that those who initially rule alongside the beast will become "of one mind, and…give their kingdom to the beast" (verse 17).

That is where the world will end up. That is the direction we are headed as Satan uses the many means at his disposal for advancing his globalist agenda.

## THE MANY FRONTS OF GLOBALISM

### Organizations with Globalist Agendas

As we go through history, we find globalist-minded groups like the Knights Templar, the Freemasons, the Rosicrucians, and others. There have been powerful banking titans and their families, like the Rothschilds and the Rockefellers, who have helped to finance organizations and programs that have globalist intents.

In 1921, a group of globalist-minded leaders founded the Council of Foreign Relations, which, for decades has had a pervasive influence. Out of slightly more than 500 government officials from 1945 to 1972, more than half were members of this council.[3] We can probably say that other than the United Nations, the Council on Foreign Relations has been among the biggest contributors to encouraging a global government. Professor Carroll Quigley of Georgetown University wrote, "The Council on Foreign Relations is the American branch of a society which originated in England [and] believes national boundaries should be obliterated and one-world rule established."[4]

Here in the United States, another contributor is the Federal Reserve, which is not federal at all. It operates independently of the US government and is the most powerful economic institution in the country. It is responsible for managing US monetary policy, and those who serve on its board of directors are selected by the president and approved by Congress. Americans have no say in the Federal Reserve's decisions. When the United States implements a central bank digital currency, it will be the Federal Reserve that determines how it is put into place.

After World War I, the League of Nations was established with the goal of preventing a world war from happening again. Their goal was to create global unity. Yet it didn't take long for World War II to break out. After the war ended in 1945, once again, an organization was created to prevent global warfare: the United Nations. Both the

League of Nations and the United Nations were created to resolve the world's problems, but those problems have not gone away.

The United Nations currently has many different agencies tasked to solve issues faced by the world. All of its efforts are globalist in nature. And the most ambitious program it has ever created is the 2030 Agenda for Sustainable Development. One of the main goals of this program is to end global poverty, and the UN has urged every one of its member nations to commit to the goals of the agenda. This, of course, calls for global cooperation, and is being mandated by a globalist organization.

Back in 1968, the Club of Rome was founded. According to its website, its goal is to "identify holistic solutions to complex global issues and promote policy initiatives and action to enable humanity to emerge from multiple planetary emergencies."[5] This organization has what it calls Earth4All, an "international initiative to accelerate the system-change we need for an equitable future on a finite planet." They warn that "the next ten years must see the fastest economic transformation in history if we want to steer humanity away from social and ecological catastrophe."[6]

The Club of Rome views the world as comprised of ten different regions based on the features and problems of those regions. When this was first announced, the prophecy world got excited, thinking perhaps this was connected in some way to the ten kingdoms mentioned in Daniel 7:24. But there are some who don't believe that to be an accurate assessment, and I agree.

### Individuals Who Advocate a World Order

In recent decades, there have been individual visionaries who have called for steps to be taken toward what would ultimately bring about a global government. Henry Kissinger was one of them. In 1994, he said, "The New World Order cannot happen without U.S. participation, as we are the most significant single component. Yes, there will be a New World Order, and it will force the United States to change its perceptions."[7]

David Rockefeller, in a private meeting in June 1991 held by the Trilateral Commission, said, "The world is now more sophisticated and prepared to march towards World Government. The supra-national sovereignty of an intellectual elite and world bankers is surely preferable to the national auto-determination practiced in past centuries."[8]

In 2003, David Rockefeller stated in his book *Memoirs*, "Some even believe we are part of a secret cabal working against the best interests of the United States, characterizing my family and me as internationalists and of conspiring with others around the world to build a more integrated global political and economic structure, One World if you will. If that's the charge, I stand guilty and I am proud of it."[9] He boldly admits that he and his family agree with the goal of establishing a global system.

Former president George Herbert Walker Bush was a proponent of a new world order as well. This was a common theme when he talked about foreign policy. In his State of the Union address in 1991, he said, "It's a big idea: a new world order, where diverse nations are drawn together in common cause to achieve the universal aspirations of mankind: peace and security, freedom and the rule of law." He then added, "Among the nations of the world, only the United States has both the moral standing and the means to back it up."[10]

No less than Pope Francis at the Vatican has been vocal about this. In an encyclical letter, he lamented the fact nations are becoming weaker, and said that "it is essential to devise stronger and more efficiently organized international institutions, with functionaries who are appointed fairly by agreement among national governments, and empowered to impose sanctions."[11] That is essentially a call for a one-world governing body. In the same letter, he said that "the limits and borders of individual states" stand in the way of human rights and dignity. In saying this, he criticizes national sovereignty.

Back in 2003, Pope John Paul II gave an address to the new ambassador of Israel to the Vatican, saying, "My pilgrimage is a pilgrimage of hope; the hope of the 21st century will lead to a new solidarity among the peoples of the world…it is precisely this hope and this concept of solidarity that must ever inspire all men and all women… in working for a new world order based on harmonious relations and effective cooperation between peoples."[12]

Billionaire George Soros has stated, "The main obstacle to a stable and just world order is the United States."[13] And in his book *Open Society: Reforming Global Capitalism*, Soros says, "It may be shocking to say, but I believe that the current unilateralist posture of the United States constitutes a serious threat to the peace and prosperity of the world."[14]

Soros is just one of many prominent billionaires who are able to exert enormous influence over what happens in our world. Their deep pockets and close connections with various governments and organizations enable them to fund and support globalist agendas.

### Movements That Urge Globalist Solutions
#### Open Borders

One example of how global elitists have affected government policies is through their advocacy of open borders. As I mentioned earlier, Europe has had to deal with an overwhelming flow of immigrants at great social, political, and economic cost. The same has been happening in the US.

The Heritage Foundation reports that in the US, "what we're seeing at the border is close collaboration and collusion between open-borders advocates within and outside of government." According to their research, there is "a large network of non-profits, non-governmental organizations, NGOs for short, down at the border [that] are acting as a massive way point and resettlement program." They say this is an international issue, with "the Open Society Foundation and George

Soros and his billions of dollars…[and] a lot more players involved…
They don't believe in territorial sovereignty or the nation state."[15]

All of this is having a destabilizing effect on Europe and the US. And
it is playing into the schemes of globalists who want to eliminate borders.

## Climate Change

Another front on which globalists are moving their agenda forward is the environmental movement. I say this cautiously because
we *should* be taking care of our environment. God gave mankind
that responsibility when He told Adam to maintain the garden of
Eden (Genesis 2:15). But today's environmental alarmists are warning that unless we make drastic energy policy and lifestyle changes,
the world will be destroyed in a few years. They say the solution is
global cooperation and government-imposed restrictions on the kinds
of energy people can and cannot use.

The idea that planet Earth has only a few years left is nonsense—
who can possibly control the climate? Only God can do that. There's
a website article titled "Doomsday Addiction: Celebrating 50 Years
of Failed Climate Predictions,"[16] which shows the many times alarmists have been wrong.

Though alarmists have repeatedly been proven incorrect, their
efforts are having a significant impact. One survey of people in the
UK revealed that "seven in 10 Brits support 'world government' to
protect humanity from global catastrophes." They are saying that
only a one-world government can fix the problem. The survey further reported that "88 per cent of respondents said they would be
prepared to make changes that would affect their living standards to
prevent catastrophic climate change in the future."[17]

A few years ago, the United Nations released a report that led to
the news headline "UN: Humans Could Cause Extinction of 1 Million Species, Globalism Will Fix." The article cited the claim that
mankind can "stop the destruction through 'transformative change'

that could translate into globalism replacing national sovereignty and nations' self-determination."[18] In other words, only globalism can save the planet. That has been the message of climate alarmists for years.

In 1996, former Soviet president Mikhail Gorbachev spoke about the strategic use of climate alarmism for globalist purposes. He said, "The threat of environmental crisis will be the international disaster key to unlock the New World Order."[19] Earlier, in 1993, Gorbachev founded Green Cross International, which now has a global network with member organizations in 30 countries. His intent was for it to serve "as an international body to respond to ecological issues and environmental problems."[20]

## THE STEPPING STONES TO THE
## ANTICHRIST'S ONE-WORLD EMPIRE

All these historic examples and quotes that I have shared here demonstrate that for thousands of years, in so many ways, mankind has schemed to bring about a global utopia, but has never been successful. One world apart from God is not God's will. The Tower of Babel was a failure, and every effort since then has failed. Mankind has a dark and sinful heart and is incapable of producing good results. Only Jesus Christ can give the world what it longs for, yet people have shut Him out of their lives. Only He can bring a global kingdom that offers true peace and is free of problems and pain.

But there is coming a day when it will appear that mankind has finally succeeded. As we already learned from Daniel 11 and Revelation 13, during the end times, the antichrist will rule the entire world. And we've looked at some of the ways governments and leaders are moving us in that direction. Some of the stepping stones that will lead to a powerful global government are with us today—socialized medicine, centralized economic systems, organizations pushing agendas that call for governing bodies vested with worldwide authority, open borders, and more. There are forces at work that are undermining the family and giving governments greater control over how future generations of children are raised. We are in danger of crises that could force nations to centralize their decision-making processes, such as a global economic collapse.

We saw the profound impact the COVID lockdowns had on our world. Governments imposed draconian restrictions on their citizens. What will happen when the next global crisis hits? Imagine what another pandemic could do. Or a worldwide financial implosion caused by the unsustainable levels of debt everywhere. Or imagine terrorists carrying out 9/11-type attacks in two dozen cities around the world simultaneously. Another world war would be catastrophic. Whatever the case, it's possible we could be one major event away from seeing people become so frightened that they say, "We need a one-world government to control this."

## THE RAPTURE AND THE NEW WORLD ORDER

One event that is certain to cause global chaos is the rapture of the church. When that happens, millions of believers will suddenly disappear, and those who are left behind will be terrified. With so many people suddenly gone, the havoc and turmoil will be devastating. It will take an enormous amount of effort and time to restore stability.

The rapture could very well be the catalyst that brings on the new world order so many have been striving for. After the rapture will come the tribulation, which the Bible calls "the time of Jacob's trouble" (Jeremiah 30:7). During this seven-year period, without the church on earth, globalists will finally get their one-world government, ruled by the antichrist. They will get their paradise, but it will be hell. Because God is pouring out judgment upon the world, conditions will become so bad that people will cry out to the mountains and rocks, "Fall on us and hide us from the face of Him who sits on the throne and from the wrath of the lamb!" (Revelation 6:16).

After thousands of years of attempts, the antichrist's empire will be the best mankind can do. Evil will be rampant and at its worst. It will be a horrific time, which is why God will spare the church from this ordeal (1 Thessalonians 1:10; 5:9; Revelation 3:10). In the antichrist's world order, every kind of wickedness will flourish. Everyone and everything will be utterly immoral and vile and corrupt because Christ has been left out of the picture.

## THE FUTILITY OF ALL SCHEMES AGAINST GOD

Scripture provides us with some perspective on the whole matter of human governments versus God. In Psalm 2:1-6, we read this:

> Why do the nations rage,
>   and the people plot a vain thing?
> The kings of the earth set themselves,
>   and the rulers take counsel together,
>   against the LORD and against His Anointed, saying,
> "Let us break Their bonds in pieces
>   and cast away Their cords from us."
> He who sits in the heavens shall laugh,
>   the Lord shall hold them in derision.
> Then He shall speak to them in His wrath,
>   and distress them in His deep displeasure:
> "Yet I have set My King
>   on My holy hill of Zion."

God is in the heavens laughing at the fools who plot vainly to take counsel against Him. Every earthly kingdom will fail. When Christ returns, He will establish His global empire in Zion, in Israel.

Ephesians 6:12 tells us who we are really battling against: "We do not wrestle against flesh and blood, but against principalities, against powers, against the rulers of the darkness of this age, against spiritual hosts of wickedness in the heavenly places." So while people are the face of the push for a global kingdom, it is the powers and rulers of darkness that are motivating them to think they can create paradise without God. But that's impossible. Every past effort has ended in ignominious defeat, and every future attempt will end the same way—including the antichrist's empire.

Psalm 37:1-2 says,

> Do not fret because of evildoers,
> nor be envious of the workers of iniquity.
> For they shall soon be cut down like the grass,
> and wither as the green herb.

The evildoers who have been plotting and scheming for thousands of years to create a one-world government apart from God have been and will be cut down. A few verses later, the psalmist says, "For yet a little while and the wicked shall be no more" (verse 10). Their efforts are in vain, and God will destroy them.

## THE GLORIOUS ONE-WORLD GOVERNMENT OF CHRIST

Now, there *is* a good one-world government coming. After the tribulation, Christ will return and set up His kingdom here on earth. He will reign for 1,000 years over what is known as the millennial kingdom (Revelation 20:4-6). He will establish His perfect global government in Jerusalem, from which He will rule all the nations. At last, the utopia only the Lord Himself can bring will be here, and wars will finally cease. The prophet Isaiah says of this time,

They shall beat their swords into plowshares,
and their spears into pruning hooks;
nation shall not lift up sword against nation,
neither shall they learn war anymore (2:4).

Even the animal kingdom will know true peace:

The wolf also shall dwell with the lamb,
the leopard shall lie down with the young goat,
the calf and the young lion and the fatling together;
and a little child shall lead them (11:6).

What a glorious time this will be!

None of mankind's attempts to bring peace and prosperity has ever worked, from the Tower of Babel to the world empires of history to the League of Nations, Council on Foreign Relations, and United Nations. That's because all of them have been and continue to be godless. You cannot succeed when God is left out. Only Christ's earthly kingdom will bring what people have longed for.

Revelation 11:15 tells us that during the tribulation, when the seventh trumpet sounds, loud voices in heaven will proclaim, "The kingdoms of this world have become the kingdoms of our Lord and of His Christ, and He shall reign forever and ever!"

Yes, the Lord Jesus Christ will reign forever and ever. His millennial kingdom on earth will last for 1,000 years, after which He will usher in the new heavens and the new earth and rule for all eternity.

God has incredible plans for the future, and we who are His children are part of those plans. We have much to look forward to—hallelujah!

CHAPTER 2

# THE PRIMACY OF JESUS CHRIST IN REVELATION

JEFF KINLEY

The book of Revelation is jam-packed with all kinds of details about what will happen during earth's final days. So much so that it's easy to be overwhelmed by it all. Yet so much of what we see happening in today's world lines up with the prophecies about this time of unrestrained sin and divine judgment. We are seeing globalists call for a one-world government, the emergence of a digital economy, apostasy infiltrating the church, the spirit of antichrist rising (a spirit present in the apostle John's day and even more so in ours), Israel being threatened by her enemies, unimaginable moral and spiritual depravity, and delusion on a scale never before known.

All of this can make the book of Revelation appear intimidating.

Yet there is one central figure that stands clearly above all others in Revelation, and that is the Lord Jesus Christ. He is the dominant theme from start to finish. It is impossible to miss the truth that He is in control over all—His sovereign hand is visible in all that happens. He is the common thread that runs through the entire book, and when our focus is on Him, the rest of the book makes better sense. He welcomes us into the book, and He promises blessing to us for reading Revelation and keeping the instructions written within it (Revelation 1:3).

The common perception many people have about Revelation is that it's the book of the Bible in which God tells us about the future. But God does that all through Scripture, beginning with Genesis. He gives revelation about Himself as well as about what is to come.

Genesis chapter 1 begins, "In the beginning God created the heavens and the earth." These ten words are packed with a lot of theology, and they reveal much about God Himself. From this passage alone there is much we can learn, starting with the truths that God is eternal and He predates His creation. The fact that He created everything tells us He is supernaturally powerful and omnipotent. This is confirmed elsewhere in the Bible, such as in Romans 1:20, which says that God's invisible attributes can be seen in His creation. He is a master architect and builder. As Psalm 19:1 says, "The heavens declare the glory of God; and the firmament shows His handiwork." And in Job 38:4, God told Job, "Where were you when I laid the foundations of the earth?" As we take a closer look at God's creation, we see that He is a God of great detail, order, and precision.

Those are among the truths and thoughts we can glean from just one verse in the Bible!

There's more we can discover in the opening words of Genesis. Back in the nineteenth century, there was an English philosopher named Herbert Spencer, who was an advocate of Darwinian thought. He determined that everything that exists fits into one of five categories: time, force, energy, space, and matter. Yet Spencer wasn't the first to figure that out. God was way ahead of him—we see those same five categories mentioned at the very beginning of the Bible!

Let's look at Genesis 1:1 again: "In the beginning" speaks of *time*. "God" is the *force* who did the creating. He "created," which represents *energy*. "The heavens" is *space*, and "the earth" is *matter*.

God had all these categories figured out before man existed.

Not only that, but the very first words of the Bible speak about science, physics, and astronomy. God informs us casually about what scientists struggle to articulate. That's why I like to say our universe began with a big God and not a big bang. It was God who divinely spoke all things into existence.

As you can see, we can learn a wealth of truths about God right from the beginning of Scripture. And over the centuries, as more of the Bible was written, God revealed more about Himself to us. He gradually turned up the lights, so to speak, so that we could learn about Him. He gave revelations about Himself to the Jewish people, who recorded the Scriptures for us. This is one of the reasons Satan hates the Jewish people so much—they gave us the Bible.

In the New Testament we come to the capstone of God's revelation: the person of Jesus Christ. The incarnation of Jesus is the ultimate revelation of God to us. Hebrews 1:3 says that Jesus "is the radiance of [God's] glory and the exact representation of His nature" (NASB). God continues to reveal more all through the New Testament, including the last book of the Bible, Revelation. Here, He gives His final written word to the church, and ultimately, to mankind. It is here we find Jesus' last words to appear in print—words we should pay attention to.

## THE PURPOSES OF REVELATION

Have you ever considered that last words are lasting words? The book of Revelation is how God chose to conclude His masterpiece of revelation to the world. There were other things God could have written, but He didn't. He didn't say, "Remember what I told you in the previous sixty-five books." He didn't say, "Make sure you keep doing what I've told you to do." Instead, He gave a revelation of the Lord Jesus Christ, through which we are told about the future, warned to avoid sin, called to be ready, and promised blessing.

### A Heads-Up About the Future

In Revelation, God gave us a book that is 95 percent Bible prophecy. Why? Because He wants to give us a heads-up on the future. He wants us to know what will happen. But beyond giving us a panorama of the end of the age, He designed for the last book of the Bible to reveal Himself and His attributes to us. For this reason, we can call Revelation God's grand finale.

### A Warning Against Apathy and Sin

Another reason God asked John to write Revelation is that in just two short generations, some in the church had drifted from Him. They weren't living as God had called them to. If they had looked at themselves in a mirror, they wouldn't have recognized themselves because of how far they had strayed from the Lord. And He certainly didn't recognize them.

### A Call to Be Ready

Still another reason for Revelation is so that the church would be ready for the rapture, and eventually, the Lord's second coming. For the church, the rapture is an imminent event—it could take place at any time. God wants His people to always be prepared.

### A Source of Blessing

We are told in Revelation 1:3, "Blessed is he who reads and those who hear the words of this prophecy, and keep those things which are written in it." If we read, hear, and obey this book, we will be blessed—and part of that blessing is getting to know our Lord in ways we didn't know of before, as revealed in Revelation.

## THE SETTING OF REVELATION

The apostle John wrote Revelation during his exile on the isle of Patmos. He had been banished there by the Roman emperor Domitian.

This small island is a ten-mile by six-mile rock in the Aegean Sea. I call it the Alcatraz of that day and region.

By this time, John is in his nineties. The early church fathers tell us he had been persecuted—he was boiled alive in oil and is said to have continued to preach the gospel even as that was happening. So here we have a man who has persevered through much. And God chooses to give him the last-ever revelation about who He is.

## THE FOCUS OF REVELATION

As we begin Revelation, we find that the Lord's top priority is to reveal Himself to us. Notice He does this *before* He explains the apocalypse, judgments, the antichrist, the second coming, the millennial kingdom, and the eternal state. And He does this in Revelation chapter 1, which isn't an introduction to Revelation, but rather, the essence of it.

As we make our way through Revelation 1, imagine yourself on an airplane, ready to view the expanse of all it tells us about the Lord. This chapter is packed densely with theology, and my encouragement is that you read through it carefully so you can examine its amazing truths and let them impact your life.

Revelation 1 opens with these profound words: "The Revelation of Jesus Christ." This book is all about Jesus. We find this affirmed a little later in verse 5, which tells us this message comes "from Jesus Christ, the faithful witness." But why does He describe Himself this way? Because everything stated in the book of Revelation is predicated on the credibility of Jesus Christ. If He is not a truth teller, how can we trust any of what is recorded for us? Also, the fact Jesus is "the faithful witness" contrasts Him with those who do not tell the truth—the antichrist, the false prophet, and Satan. Remember, in John 8:44, Jesus called Satan "a liar and the father of it."

Jesus Himself proclaimed, "I am the way, the truth, and the life" (John 14:6). He is reliable and trustworthy. In a culture that is drowning in a sea of lies, we can rely on Him to give us absolute, undiluted truth.

Going back to Revelation 1:5, we read that Jesus is "the firstborn from the dead." The word used in the original Greek text is *prototokos*, which means "preeminent one, first in line, heir to the throne." He was resurrected in a way unlike anyone else has ever been raised up. He is above all others, which makes sense because He goes on to say He is "ruler over the kings of the earth."

Later, in Revelation 19:16, we read that Jesus is "King of kings and Lord of lords." He is the almighty. There is no one greater. No one compares. In Isaiah 40, the Lord's greatness is described at length. In verse 7, we read, "The grass withers, the flower fades, because the breath of the LORD blows upon it; surely the people are grass." Verse 24 picks up again on this theme, saying: "When He will also blow on them, and they will wither, and the whirlwind will take them away like stubble." All the Lord has to do is blow on people, and like dust, they will be scattered in the wind. Even the rulers of the earth are nothing to Him (Isaiah 40:23-25).

Revelation 1:5 then describes Jesus as "Him who loved us and washed us from our sins in His own blood." He is our Redeemer. He possesses a loyal, faithful, and unconditional love for us. He will never let go of us. His love for us is so complete that He will never love us more than He does now. We are covered and protected by Him. This is such an amazing truth that we can't help but stop ourselves for a few moments and contemplate it. The God of the universe loves me!

This is not some cold truth that sits on the page of a book. We experience His love in very real ways. So great is His love that He released us from our sin by shedding His blood on the cross. Through His unimaginable sacrifice, He broke the power and penalty of sin in our lives. Sin no longer has authority or dominion over us. Christ has enabled us to overcome sin, and there is coming a day when we will be freed from the presence of sin—all because Jesus loves us.

However, Jesus did a lot more for us. Revelation 1:6 says He "has made us kings and priests to His God and Father." This mean we no longer have to go through a human priest—as the ancient Israelites did—for our sins to be forgiven and for us to have access to God. Hebrews 4:16 says we can now "come boldly to the throne of grace, that we may obtain mercy and find grace to help in time of need." We can draw near to God with confidence, knowing that because of what Christ did for us, we will always receive grace and mercy. We will never be condemned or rejected. We might be disciplined, but we won't be punished.

John's next words in Revelation 1:6 are a perfect response to all of what Christ has done for us: "to Him be glory and dominion forever and ever. Amen." The astounding truths about what Christ has made possible for us should inspire us to worship. In fact, the book of Revelation is so packed with truths about what Christ has done that there are more than a dozen doxologies, or worship scenes, within its pages. As we study the Lord's character and actions, we cannot help but say, "I must worship Him!"

Next, John tells us Christ will return. In Revelation 1:7, he writes, "Behold, He is coming with clouds, and every eye will see Him, even they who pierced Him. And all the tribes of the earth will mourn because of Him." We know this refers to the second coming because of the fact everyone will see Him. That won't happen at the rapture, during which we will be taken up and meet the Lord in the air (1 Thessalonians 4:17).

At the second coming, Christ will come to the earth. He will be visible, and His return will be a global event—it will be witnessed by every living soul on planet Earth. And in contrast to the rapture, when He is welcomed by believers who are taken to heaven, the unbelievers who witness His second coming will experience great terror and dread. They will mourn because their fate is judgment.

Still another characteristic we learn about our Lord in Revelation 1 is that He is unrivaled. He has no equals. Jesus said in verse 8, "I am the Alpha and Omega, the Beginning and the End...who is and who was and who is to come, the Almighty."

The words *alpha* and *omega* are the first and last letters of the Greek alphabet—they are the beginning and the end, or the bookends. This means Jesus is the sum total of all knowledge. If you want to know what life is all about, don't look for the answers from the world, but from Him. Colossians 2:3 affirms this, saying that in Christ are found "all the treasures of wisdom and knowledge."

Christ is also the one who reveals. In Revelation 1:11, the Lord says to John, "What you see, write in a book." Jesus makes it clear He will reveal information meant to be written down for all time. This brings us to an important point: One of the most persistent myths about the book of Revelation is it is some kind of hidden, cryptic book that is hard to understand. But the very name of the book dispels that: It is "the Revelation of Jesus Christ." The words John was asked to write are not meant to hide truth, but to reveal it. Revelation is not a code to be deciphered; rather, it is filled with teachings for us to know and believe.

There is much we can understand in Revelation when we take the words in their most literal, plain meaning. Even much of the symbolic language can be figured out when we read the context carefully or study the Old Testament passages that are quoted in Revelation. For example, the supposedly mysterious "seven stars" we see in Christ's right hand in Revelation 1:16 are revealed to be "the angels [messengers or pastors] of the seven churches" in verse 20.

## THE CHRIST OF REVELATION

At Revelation 1:12, the airplane we're riding banks into a turn. In the next several verses, John writes about a remarkable vision he has. We're about to see a side of Jesus that too few people talk about—the risen, glorified, exalted Lord Jesus Christ.

### He Is Righteous

First, in verse 13, we are introduced to Christ's righteousness. Jesus is seen standing in the middle of seven lampstands, and He is "clothed with a garment down to the feet and girded about the chest with a golden band." This garment is the equivalent of what the high priests wore in the Old Testament. The high priest's role was to be a righteous representative of the people before God. He stood before God on everyone else's behalf.

But from the time of the cross onward, Jesus has been the final high priest. It is His righteousness that enables Him to stand on our behalf for God. When we come to Christ as our Savior and Lord, we become partakers of His righteousness, which is imputed to us. As 2 Corinthians 5:21 says, "He made Him who knew no sin to be sin for us, that we might become the righteousness of God in Him." This is what it means for us to be clothed with the righteousness of Christ.

John then says that Jesus' "head and hair were white like wool, as white as snow" (Revelation 1:14). John wasn't merely describing the color of Jesus' hair. This glowing, brilliant aspect of Jesus' appearance reveals His wisdom and glory. As Proverbs 16:31 says, "The silver-haired head is a crown of glory." Christ is the supernatural sage of the ages. Revelation 1:14 continues, "His eyes [were] like a flame of fire." This speaks of Christ's penetrating gaze into the human heart. His laser-like vision is able to see past our actions and into our thoughts and motives.

A few years ago, I had the privilege of helping to write *Gifted Mind*, the autobiography of Dr. Raymond Damadian, the man who invented and built the first MRI scanner. I spent a lot of time with him and ended up learning far more about science and the MRI scanner than I could have imagined. I was awed by the capabilities of this scanner—it sees more than an X-ray machine sees. It can scan everything within you, even to the point of discerning the liquids in your body. Nothing is hidden from this imaging device. That's how it is with Jesus—He sees everything. His flaming eyes can see all there is to know about the church and us. It is His ability to discern every thought and motive that enables Him to both commend and rebuke the seven churches mentioned in Revelation chapters 2–3. His piercing gaze continues to examine our hearts today, and will equip Him to judge the lost at His second coming and the great white throne judgment.

### He Is a Refiner

We next learn that Christ is the one who refines: "His feet were like fine brass, as if refined in a furnace" (Revelation 1:15). This pictures Jesus' role as judge. His refining work is one of exercising divine judgment, which He will someday pour out on the world. And in Revelation 2–3, Jesus also refines the church. He desires for His followers to purge sin from their lives. This refining work is applied to every one of us, which is why Scripture so frequently admonishes us to have pure hearts.

### He Is a Reprover

Next, John tells us Christ is a reprover. Back in Revelation 1:10, John heard Jesus' "loud voice, as of a trumpet." Here in verse 15, we read that "His voice [is] as the sound of many waters." Water can be powerful and majestic. Think about the crashing of waves upon coastal rocks—the waves are constant, and their remarkable strength commands respect. John would have heard such waves on the isle of Patmos, making it likely this was what he had in mind when he described Christ's voice. Our Lord speaks with resounding authority and credibility.

Verse 16 adds that "out of [Christ's] mouth went a sharp two-edged sword." This speaks of the Word of God, which Hebrews 4:12 describes as a two-edged sword. It's important for us to note that in the New Testament, there are two Greek words translated "sword."

One is *macharia* (Hebrews 4:12), and the other is *rhomphaia*, which refers to a long, broad sword, like a *Braveheart* sword. The latter is the word John used here in Revelation 1:15 and later in 19:15. At Armageddon, Christ will use His sword to judge and slaughter all His enemies. But here in Revelation 1, He is preparing to perform surgery on His churches. His words are about to cut into the seven congregations He writes to in Revelation 2–3 for the purpose of revealing what's really going on in the lives of believers and their churches. He wants to open their collective hearts for the purpose of healing and restoring them.

Jesus' Word continues its piercing work today through pastor-teachers who are faithful to preach the Bible, even when it is not popular to do so. Their diligence is needed more critically than ever, for in these last days, many are departing from the faith, paying attention to myths and doctrines of demons (1 Timothy 4:1-2).

### He Is Radiant

Revelation 1:16 goes on to say that Christ's "countenance was like the sun shining in its strength." He is the *radiant* Christ. The glory that emanates from Jesus is extraordinarily brilliant. Imagine what it's like to look at the sun, which we cannot do because it would burn our corneas and cause us to go blind. But by comparing our Lord's countenance to the sun, John gives us some idea of how brightly Christ's glory shines.

Too often when we envision Jesus, we think of Him as the humble carpenter, the one who died on the cross, the one who washed the disciples' feet. But Jesus is now risen and glorified. Here in Revelation 1, John sees the Lord in the fullness of His splendor and majesty.

### He Is to Be Revered

This stunning vision of Christ overwhelmed John. In Revelation 1:17 we see the apostle's response: "When I saw Him, I fell at His feet as dead." John trembled in fear and humility. He was unable look directly at Jesus. He knew he was standing before exalted deity. His reaction was similar to that of the prophet Isaiah when he was taken, in a vision, to God's throne room: "Woe is me, for I am undone! Because I am a man of unclean lips…for my eyes have seen the King, the LORD of hosts" (Isaiah 6:5). For John, seeing Christ in the fullness of His holiness was faith-inspiring and traumatic.

Tragically, this is not the Christ we read or hear about most of the time today. It's not the Christ presented in many pulpits or books. Revelation 1 reminds us that the Jesus who now resides in heaven is exalted, intimidating, transcendent, holy, and eminently worthy of our worship.

### He Is Reassuring

Upon seeing John fall before Him, Jesus "laid His right hand" on John, and said, "Do not be afraid; I am the First and the Last. I am He who lives, and was dead, and behold, I am alive forevermore" (Revelation 1:17-18).

Again, this is the Christ who we follow and worship. He is a living, risen Lord. No other religious leader has ever risen from the grave. All the others have rotted and turned to dust. But Jesus sits exalted at the right hand of the Father. That is why He alone is worthy of all reverence and worship.

Yet at the same time, He gives comfort and assurance to His own. In this tender moment, as John lays prostrate on the ground in reverent fear, Jesus lovingly lays His right hand on John and says, "Do not be afraid."

But there is another way Christ offers assurance to John. He adds, "I have the keys of Hades and Death" (verse 18). This is another way of saying, "Satan and his minions will no longer have any power in the afterlife." Christ is the Lord over hell. There is coming a day when the struggles of this world will end, and Satan and all those who follow him will receive their just and eternal condemnation.

## THE OUTLINE OF REVELATION

After Jesus reassures John, He tells the apostle to pick up a pen and gives these instructions: "Write the things which you have seen [the past], and the things which are [the present], and the things which will take place after this [the future]" (verse 19). This is the outline of the entire book of Revelation. John would go on to catalog the last-ever prophecy given before Jesus returns for His bride at the rapture. John would write about the vision he had just seen, pen Jesus' letters to the seven churches that were present at the time in Asia Minor, then give a stunning glimpse into the future, providing details about the tribulation, Christ's millennial kingdom on earth, and heaven and eternity.

## THE RESPONSE TO REVELATION

All through Revelation 1, we are given a stunning portrayal of the risen, living Christ as He is now. This raises an important question: Is this the Christ you know? Is this the one you have been worshipping? Or do you have a different image of Christ in mind—one that doesn't portray Him as He truly is?

How we view God determines everything about us. Therefore, Scripture's descriptions of Christ must be what inform and influence our vision of Jesus. Only when we see Christ as He truly is will we have a right response to Him. How could we possibly see this Christ in all His authority and power and glory, and yet remain the same?

So when we read the book of Revelation, we are reading about the Lord Jesus Christ. We also learn that the key to understanding prophecy in the end times is to know Him. In this final book of the Bible, there is much we learn about who He is and what He does. He is the head of the church. After He brings judgment, He will rule from His throne in Jerusalem. We will have an incredible future with Him in the millennial kingdom and the new heavens and new earth.

Revelation tells us Jesus is holy, wise, sovereign, and that He will be victorious. In fact, He is far more glorious and wonderful than we can ever imagine.

Prophecy begins and ends with Jesus Christ. The first prophecy in the Bible appears in Genesis 3:15. There, we read about how the seed of the woman is going to crush the head of the serpent. And in the last prophecy, in Revelation 22:20, Jesus declares, "Surely I am coming quickly."

As we walk the tightrope of our day—a day that is getting worse as we head quickly toward the end times—it is sometimes difficult to know what we should believe or do. But through Revelation, our Lord says, "Keep your eyes on Me. Look up, not down." Like Peter when he walked on water, we must keep our eyes on Jesus to keep from sinking.

The Jesus of Revelation lovingly admonishes us not to be afraid. So don't be dismayed by what is taking place all around us. Instead, look to Him. He is watching over you, and He will take care of you. Keep your eyes fixed on Him. And let everything you learn and know about Him fill you with strength, confidence, peace, and hope.

# CHAPTER 3

# PERILOUS TIMES: WHEN AMERICA ABANDONS THE ROLE OF GLOBAL LEADERSHIP

## MICHELE BACHMANN

I n recent history, there is one important event that has changed everything for Christians: the rebirth of the nation of Israel. Beginning in the late nineteenth century, the Jewish people moved back to their ancestral homeland in large numbers, and the Hebrew language was revived. The valley of dry bones described in Ezekiel 37—which we are told is "the whole house of Israel"—started coming to life (verses 1-14).

Scripture tells us that the rebirth of Israel is the one event that sets the stage for the last days and Christ's return. Israel became a nation again in 1948, and this miracle defines the times that we live in. That's why it is imperative that we understand what is happening and know how we should live.

I came to know Jesus Christ when I was 16 years of age, and my life changed completely. The difference was dramatic—almost like the way the movie *The Wizard of Oz* started out in black and white and then all of a sudden went to technicolor. That's how I felt when I came to know Christ. It's this transformation that explains why those who know Christ put their faith into everything they do.

When we come to Christ, the Lord lifts a veil from our understanding and, through the Holy Spirit, opens the Word of God for us. He enables us to comprehend His truth in ways that our natural mind cannot. The Lord reveals His words and thoughts to us and infuses us with what He wants us to know. And He equips us with a faith that is able to be active and go on the offense. Christianity is not a faith that cowers in the corner or apologizes for what it says. Rather, Christianity is a faith meant to be on the move.

In America's history we see a wonderful example of Christianity on the march. Who we are as a nation was shaped by the fact many of our first settlers knew Christ and the Bible. As we compare the past to what is happening today, we will come to realize the extent of the grand larceny taking place in America. We are seeing the theft of a rich legacy built by prior generations who made great sacrifices as they stood on the shoulders of giants in the faith. It's as we look to our history that we will realize the seriousness of what is happening today.

## THE SPREAD OF CHRISTIANITY
## AROUND THE WORLD

During the first century AD, Christianity spread to the region now known as France and to North Africa. It continued to spread, reaching to what is now Tunisia, Algeria, and Sri Lanka. During the second century AD, the gospel reached as far as what is now Portugal and Morocco, followed by Austria, Switzerland, and Belgium. By the fourth century AD, the gospel reached Ethiopia. Almost 200 years later, Pope Gregory I sent Augustine of Canterbury to what is now England. Many ended up receiving Christ and being baptized in a land that had been deeply pagan. Near the middle of the seventh century AD, the first Christian missionaries arrived in China. In the early eighth century, the gospel reached Norway, which I am glad for because I am 100 percent Norwegian. And near the end of the tenth century, Christianity spread to Iceland.

By around 1200, the Bible was available in 22 different languages.[1] In 1491, missionaries arrived at what is now the African Congo—then a short while later, Kenya. In Spain, Pope Alexander VI sent Catholic missionaries to the New World on one of Columbus's journeys to the Americas.

In 1556, John Calvin made arrangements for French pastors to reach the people of Brazil. In the early 1600s, the Pilgrims came to North America from Holland. In the 1730s and 1740s came the Great Awakening, during which George Whitefield and Jonathan Edwards stirred revivals throughout the American colonies and the church flourished.

## THE INFLUENCE OF
## CHRISTIANITY ON AMERICA

That's how quickly the Christian faith moved mountains. I am so proud of our country's Christian heritage, which has energized me in wonderful ways. God gave us a magnificent nation, and my favorite people in our history are the Pilgrims, who were originally persecuted in England.

That persecution spurred them to travel across the English Channel and go to Holland. They lived and toiled there for many years, thinking they would be able to practice their faith in peace. That's what Scripture says we are to do—to "lead a quiet and peaceable life in all godliness and reverence" (1 Timothy 2:2).

Yet in time, Holland became the center of all the pleasures and temptations of life. The Christians who had left England could see that they and their children were vulnerable to the attractions of the world. It became difficult for them to keep body and soul together. As they met together and prayed earnestly, God laid upon the hearts of some of them to move to the New World.

In 1607, a small group of English settlers, led by Anglican priest Rev. Robert Hunt, established the first permanent English settlement in Jamestown, Virginia. By faith, the settlers brought a large wooden cross with them to plant in the sandy beaches of what is present-day Virginia Beach, Virginia, after a two-day period of self-examination, repentance, prayer, and fasting aboard ship. Rev. Hunt prayed that day, April 29, 1607, that the gospel of Jesus Christ would go forth from what is now Virginia Beach across the entire new land, and across the world.

Later, one of these English settlers, John Rolfe, married Pocahontas, the Indian princess. In the rotunda of the US Capitol is a huge historic painting that captures the most important event in Pocahontas's life. When she came to a saving knowledge of Jesus Christ, she sought to be baptized. She was taken to England, where she was baptized, and she changed her name to Rebecca, a Christian name, and spent the remainder of her days living out her faith and bringing the gospel to everyone she knew. That painting is one among others that depict the pillars on which the United States was built.

These pillars represent a background of profound faith in Jesus Christ. They portray brave people who formed the foundation of a new country in which Christianity flourished. Among them were the pilgrims who left Holland and came to North America on the *Mayflower* in 1620.

One of the passengers was William Bradford, who went on to serve as the governor of the Plymouth Colony for many years. During that time, he wrote a journal that is now the most famous account of the Pilgrims in early America. After he wrote the journal, it made its way to Boston, then went missing during the Revolutionary War.

The journal didn't surface again until decades later, and it was put into print in 1856 and is commonly known as *Of Plymouth Plantation*.

I love the Pilgrims so much because they embody the spirit of America. If you've ever asked any of the following questions, the answer, in large part, is because of the Pilgrims: What made America different from other nations? Why are we a republic in which we get to vote for our leaders rather than be subjects of a king? Why do we have a free market economy? Why do we have a unique legal and political system unlike any in the world? How did all this come about?

The roots of what we are today began with our Pilgrim fathers. They understood the Word of God, and they saw themselves as being like the children of Israel as they journeyed to a new land, living faithfully according to the principles God revealed to them. In saying this, I'm not talking about replacement theology, which teaches that the church has replaced Israel—that's not what the Bible teaches. The Pilgrims saw themselves as responsible for following God and bringing the gospel to sinners in a fallen world.

I want to give you a taste of what was in the hearts of our forefathers who came to North America by sharing some thoughts recorded in *Of Plymouth Plantation*:

> When they were ready to depart, they had a day of solemn humiliation [fasting and praying], their pastor taking his text from Ezra viii., 21: "And there at the river, by Ahava, I proclaimed a fast that we might humble ourselves before our God, and seek of Him a right way for us and for our children, and for all our substance."[2]

You see, the Pilgrims were forward-looking people. They didn't think only about their own comfort and needs. In their mind's eye, they looked ahead to "our children" and knew that there were generations of people yet unborn, including us.

Bradford, in his journal, wrote that they saw themselves as privileged to bring the gospel. They humbly viewed themselves as stepping stones and were willing to lay the foundations that would enable others to go forward faithfully. They saw themselves as accountable to transfer the gospel from one generation to the next in the same way that Paul told Timothy to do when he wrote, "The things that you have heard from me among many witnesses, commit these to faithful men who will be able to teach others also" (2 Timothy 2:2).

By the Holy Spirit's impetus, the Pilgrims saw that God had led them to come to this land and faithfully transfer the gospel to others and for generations yet unborn. Do you see why I love these people? Going back to Bradford's journal:

> Upon this discourse [the pastor] spent a good part of
> the day very profitably. The rest of the time was spent in
> pouring out prayers to the Lord with great fervency and
> abundance of tears.[3]

They knew they could very easily die on this journey. They knew that unless God was with them, they wouldn't even make it. They knew they would never come back to Holland again—ever. Everything was on the line for them. With their departure in mind, Bradford wrote,

> So they left that good and pleasant city, which had been
> their resting place for nearly twelve years; but they knew
> they were pilgrims, and lifted their eyes up to the heavens,
> their dearest country, and quieted their spirits.[4]

In the same way that God told Abram to become a pilgrim and live in tents and keep moving, they saw themselves as pilgrims who looked not at the things that they were leaving behind, but instead, up to heaven, their dearest country. This brings to mind what Hebrews chapter 11 says about Abraham, Sarah, and other Old Testament greats of the faith:

> These all died in faith, not having received the promises, but having seen them afar off were assured of them, embraced them and confessed that they were strangers and pilgrims on the earth…But now they desire a better, that is, a heavenly country. Therefore God is not ashamed to be called their God, for He has prepared a city for them (verses 13, 16).

Bradford then continued,

> When they came to the place, they found the ship and everything ready, and such of their friends as could not come with them followed them, and several came from Amsterdam to see them shipped and to take their leave of them. That night there was little sleep for most of them, for it was spent in friendly entertainment and Christian discourse and other real expressions of true Christian love. The next day the wind being fair they went aboard and their friends with them, and truly doleful was the sight of that sad and mournful parting. What sighs and sobs and prayers rose from amongst them! What tears gushed from every eye, and pithy speeches pierced each heart! Many of the Dutch strangers who stood on the quay as spectators, could not refrain from tears. Yet it was comfortable and sweet to see such lively and true expressions of dear and unfeigned love. But the tide which stays for no man called them away, though loth to depart; and their reverent pastor, falling down on his knees, and all with him, with watery cheeks commended them with most fervent prayers to the Lord and His blessing. Then with mutual embraces and

many tears, they took their leave one of another, which proved to be the last leave for many of them.[5]

I include this because what I just described is featured in one of the paintings that hangs in the US Capitol rotunda. The painting features John Robinson, the Pilgrims' pastor, who couldn't leave and go with them. He deputized other men to be their pastors because he had to stay behind with the congregation in Holland.

In the painting, everyone on the ship is looking up to heaven. They have a Bible open before them, they are crying out to God, and their emotions are clearly evident—they know what they are leaving behind. On the sail of the ship are three words: God with us.

## THE KEY TO AMERICA'S GREATNESS

It was by faith that the Pilgrim fathers came to North America. They were able to do it because God was with them. And they helped form the foundation of this country. There are more paintings that tell a Christian story, but the ones I've already described make it clear that the first settlers had a strong Christian focus. Don't believe those who claim the nation's forefathers were secularists looking to get rich. After the first Pilgrims arrived in 1620, many more came. Some helped to found Harvard College in 1636, and one of their purposes for starting the school was to train pastors who could spread the gospel of Jesus Christ.

Yale and Princeton were also founded for similar reasons. When Yale was founded in 1701, its purpose was stated as follows: "To plant, and under ye Divine blessing to propagate in this Wilderness, the blessed Reformed, Protestant Religion, in ye purity of its Order, and Worship."[6] Princeton began after the Great Awakening and its founders were ministers who said their "great intention was to erect a seminary for educating ministers of the Gospel."[7]

Within the US Capitol are many evidences of the price that the nation's forefathers paid for our liberty. They designed for the United States to be unlike any other country in the world. Leaders do not typically set up countries to enjoy freedom. The way of man is to enslave others and wield power over them. But because many of the early settlers were Christians, and because they knew the Scriptures and that Christ had come to set us free, they laid a foundation that made the US the most unique nation in all of history. The freedoms we enjoy have made it possible for our country to flourish and be of benefit to the rest of the world.

One feature of how the US was set up is that the House of Representatives has the power of the purse—the power of taxation. I'm familiar with how this works because I'm a former federal tax litigation attorney. One thing I learned in my tax training is that the power to tax can all too easily become the power to destroy. This is why it is so important that we be careful about who we send to Congress. These men and women have the legal right to take your money from you. And what we see happening today with taxes has strayed far from the Founding Fathers' intent.

There is another noteworthy work of art that hangs at the Capitol. It is in the chamber where the members of the House of Representatives meet. If you stand at the lectern where the president gives his State of the Union speech and look straight ahead, you will see a double-door entryway. Right above those doors is a marble relief portrait of Moses, the greatest lawgiver of all time.

There are other marble relief portraits in the room featuring other lawmakers throughout history. But all of them feature those lawmakers with half-profiles that look in the direction of Moses, who alone appears as a full-face relief. No other lawmaker is shown with their full face—only Moses, who is at the center of the room. Why? Because the Ten Commandments are the basis of all American and British law.

Sir William Blackstone, who wrote *Commentaries on the Law of England*, said,

> Man, considered as a creature, must necessarily be subject to the laws of his Creator... This law of nature being coeval with mankind, and dictated by God himself, is of course superior in obligation to any other. It is binding over all the globe, in all countries, and at all time: no human laws are of any validity if contrary to this.[8]

In this way, Blackstone acknowledged God as the ultimate giver of laws, which were given through Moses. Our laws descend from the Ten Commandments, from God's law. That is our heritage and legacy, which is unprecedented.

The US Constitution is the world's longest-surviving written charter of government. Though we are still a relatively young country, the Constitution is the longest-existing document of its kind. I believe that is because it was built upon God's laws and values. But today, we are seeing an unraveling of the nation's commitment to the Constitution, as well as to our laws. We are living in perilous times, which the Bible warns us about. We are living in days that the prophets foretold.

## A FAITH THAT GOES ON THE OFFENSE, NOT THE DEFENSE

While we see frightening events taking place all around us, for Christians, these are not fearful days. Though the world is falling apart, God is in control and His plans are on track. Ours is an offensive faith, not defensive. We're to be proactive as salt and light.

When I became a member of Congress, I did so because I felt the Lord calling me to go there. I ran for president several years ago for the same reason—I felt the Lord wanted to use me. And I went on the offense, asking the Lord to lead me. In Congress, I was able to have a voice in foreign policy, national security, and intelligence. That involved dealing with the nation's classified secrets, including issues our country faced in relation to terrorism. I am grateful to the Lord for giving me the privilege of having a role in those areas because as we dealt with the rise of terrorism, I was reminded of what Scripture says about the future. There were times I would be amazed at how today's events line up with what we find in God's Word.

There is so much happening around us that it's hard to keep up with it all. Jesus talked about how the signs of the end times will be like birth pains (Matthew 24:8). At first, they are far apart. But we are seeing those pains come closer together. We are getting nearer to our Lord's return. While I was in Congress, I was given access to classified secrets, and I will never disclose what I heard or read. But there was no question that the world's problems were becoming more intense, rising to levels we had never seen before.

## THE WAYS IN WHICH
## OUR WORLD IS CHANGING

Through the ages, different empires have had a dominant role over the known world. In more recent centuries, France, Spain, and England were major powers. Since World War II, the US has been the world's leading military and economic power, for the good of the entire globe. But we are seeing that change. The United Nations is working to secure global cooperation for its 2030 Agenda for Sustainable Development. The World Economic Forum has also developed what it calls Agenda 2030, which, according to its website, calls for "global unanimity."[9]

In these ways, we are seeing a select few elites play kingmakers— they are calling for a kind of cooperation that places everyone under one big system run by a few individuals. They are doing this under the banner of peace, but the underlying ideology is Marxist and advocates income equity for all, which requires a redistribution of wealth. They also push for the erasing of national borders and the elimination of national sovereignty, saying that everything would be so much better if the world was run by one global body.

But as we've seen, that won't work. For several decades, the UN hasn't been able to get much right. Some of their actions have been disastrous. For example, the UN's human rights commission has been headed up by representatives from some of the most oppressive and authoritarian nations in the world. When it comes to solving problems, it is organizations like the Samaritan's Purse that have made a real difference and provided help at a level where it is truly needed.

In terms of having a positive influence globally, we are seeing the US drop the baton. And countries like Russia, China, and Iran are picking up the baton because they want to exercise power over what is happening internationally. For years, these three countries have worked aggressively to strengthen their grip over the Middle East, while the US has withdrawn in some places and is being pushed out in others. Look at what is happening in Syria. Russia and Iran have built up their military presence, and there is pressure on the US to leave.

Russia has been on the march for a while. Putin took Georgia in 2008, invaded the Crimean Peninsula in 2014, then invaded Ukraine in 2022. China has become more aggressive in the South China Sea and poses a serious threat to its neighbors. Iran is the world's leading supporter of terrorism, and all its proxies are on the march throughout the Middle East. The Pax Americana that for so long kept the world at peace has diminished and is leaving a vacuum for others to fill.

As Islamic jihadists have spread, they've kidnapped, enslaved, raped, and killed innocent Christians in the Middle East and North Africa. Christians are being exterminated. And Iran is determined to destroy Israel. In 2015, the Ayatollah Ali Khamenei said Israel won't survive the next 25 years.[10] But too many people don't take this threat seriously, even though Khamenei and other Iranian leaders consistently call for death to Israel and the US. Iran is serious—we know this because of the fervency with which they build weapons and seek to create nuclear bombs. Their desire is to dominate the Middle East—and the world.

China is playing the long game. The Chinese Communist Party has been flying under the radar and has quietly built a massive military as well as an impressive nuclear arsenal. China now boasts the largest naval fleet in the world, which has the potential to disrupt the more than "80% of world trade [that] travels through the South China Sea."[11]

The US has been reluctant to do anything about Russia, China, and Iran because our national leaders are afraid to make them mad. Instead, the strategy is diplomatic talks, which isn't working out well, is it? Russia's answer is to take territory. China's answer is to steal trade secrets and to do cyber espionage to the tune of many billions of dollars annually.[12] And China is making major investments in Iran in exchange for the opportunity to buy large quantities of oil that evade the sanctions placed on Iran.

Tragically, there is a pervasive delusion in the US and the Western world that has enabled countries like Russia, China, and Iran to be enriched and empowered in recent years, in spite of the fact restrictions or sanctions have been placed on them. Worse yet, all three of those nations are serious nuclear threats. Do you think the US will ever do anything substantial to push back against these imminent dangers? It doesn't look likely.

Even in the past instances when the US has attempted to disarm rogue nations, the results have not been good. After the US took military action in Iraq, Libya, and Syria, what happened? All three were overtaken by various Islamic State and Al-Qaeda terrorist groups.

Back in 2012, I met privately with Israeli prime minister Benjamin Netanyahu, and I talked to him about my concerns relating to the Middle East. I urged him to take matters into his own hands and do what was necessary to protect Israel from Iran. I said that because I believed the United States could not be counted on to have Israel's back. A few years later—on July 20, 2015, the US, along with other countries, entered into a nuclear deal with Iran that ended up allowing Iran's nuclear program to continue. Since then, Iran has increased its capabilities to develop weapons-grade uranium.

In a sane world, a nation that supposedly cares about freedom and security would make it more difficult for madmen to get their hands on weapons of death.

## THE BEST USE OF OUR TIME AS PILGRIMS

Yes, we live in perilous times. And persecution is going to come. That's why it is more urgent than ever that we, as Christians, make ourselves right before the Lord. We're to live quiet and peaceful lives and spread the gospel. We're to keep in mind that we are pilgrims, and the world we live in will fade away. Heaven is our home, and we're not there yet. We will arrive there someday. But for now, we're to proclaim the gospel, which is the only source of freedom, wholeness, and peace in a world dying from sin.

What better use of our time could there be?

# CHAPTER 4

# OUR BLESSED HOPE: THE RAPTURE OF THE CHURCH

### MARK HITCHCOCK

**B**ack in 1970, the book *The Late Great Planet Earth* came out. A good number of the young people at the church I attended read the book, and as a result, there was a lot of buzz about prophecy and events that were happening around the world.

I was about 12 or 13 years old when I read the book. By that time, it had already been out for a while. I was mesmerized by the fact that the world we lived in seemed to be predicted in the Bible. It was possible to see how God was setting the stage for the end times to take place. I was excited about what I read, but because I was still young, I don't recall how much I understood of what I was reading. But the book had a deep impact on my life.

Not long after that, a movie called *The Thief in the Night* came out. I first saw it at our church one evening on one of those old reel-to-reel projectors. The acting in the movie wasn't all that good, but the message it communicated was serious.

In the movie, there are Christians who tell others about prophetic events, including the rapture and the Lord's coming. At the end, there's a scene in which a pastor is mowing his yard. The camera then moves away for a moment, then turns back—and the lawnmower is still running, but the pastor is gone. In another scene, a man is shaving in a bathroom as he talks with his wife, who is in their bedroom. Suddenly, the man is no longer responding to what his wife says. She gets up, looks in the bathroom, and sees the electric razor sitting in the sink, still buzzing.

As I watched the movie, it hit me for the first time that the rapture is a real event that will take place someday. Those who know the Lord will suddenly disappear all over the world. I still remember the effect the movie had on me as I left church that night. Since then, the truthfulness of the rapture and Bible prophecy has had an indelible impact upon my life.

About a week later, another impressionable experience took place. One day when I arrived home from school, my mom wasn't in the house. Normally she was always at home, along with my brother or sister. But I didn't see her anywhere in the house or the yard. That's when I suddenly began to wonder if maybe I had missed the rapture. I was already a believer at the time, but I was still young, and I didn't yet know the truths about the security of a believer's salvation.

Then I got the idea to call my dad at his office. I figured that if he wasn't there, then I had probably missed the rapture. Just as I was about to call, my family entered the house. They had all been next door with our neighbor. I was relieved, but the experience awakened me to the reality of what will happen when the rapture takes place.

The doctrine of the rapture is one of my favorite topics to teach about. There are two reasons for this: One, as Titus 2:13 says, the rapture is our blessed hope. In John 14:1-3, Jesus promised He would take us up from this world to be with Him in heaven. If our hope is in politics, human leaders, ourselves, or in anything other than Christ and His coming, it is ill-founded. And two, I believe the rapture is the next great event on God's prophetic calendar. The tribulation and second coming are still in the future, but before those take place, we will be raptured. Because we don't know when the rapture will happen, and because it will not be preceded by any warnings, it's important that we always be ready.

I have two goals for this chapter: The first is to examine what the rapture is all about. And the second is to talk about its place on God's prophetic time line. While we don't know the day or hour it will happen, we can look at whether the rapture will take place before, during, or after the tribulation, or if there will be a partial rapture. As we do this, I will share why I hold to the pre-trib rapture view. This view is coming under attack more and more these days, and I want to share why I believe this view is the most valid.

As we explore the rapture, I want to make it clear that the view a Christian holds regarding the rapture is not a salvation issue. There are wonderful, dedicated believers who hold to each of the different views, and we shouldn't let our persuasions about these views have a negative effect on our fellowship.

What I *will* point out, however, is that the view we hold to will affect our outlook on the future. There's a huge difference between believing we will be raptured and miss the tribulation, as opposed to believing we will go through the tribulation and face the horrors of that time.

## WHAT IS THE RAPTURE?

Let's start by looking at the definition of the word *rapture*. The term refers to the translation of living believers to heaven in a moment of time without experiencing death. While Christians who have died during the church age will be taken up at the time of the rapture, they will actually be resurrected. The rapture is for living saints and the resurrection is for deceased saints. The two groups will be raised up by our Lord in one event.

The distinction is that the rapture involves the translation of living believers' bodies, souls, and spirits into a glorified state in a very brief moment of time, whereas the resurrection raises the bodies of dead saints and reunites them to their souls and spirits—and they, too, will be in a glorified state.

### The Reason for Addressing the Rapture

There are three major New Testament texts that describe and explain the rapture: John 14:1-3, 1 Corinthians 15:51-58, and 1 Thessalonians 4:13-18. In this chapter, we're going to focus on 1 Thessalonians 4:13-18. As we do so, we'll learn some background information about the rapture, and we'll also examine what this passage tells us about the timing of this event.

Paul began with these words: "I do not want you to be ignorant, brethren, concerning those who have fallen asleep, lest you sorrow as others who have no hope" (verse 13). Notice his purpose here: He wanted to eliminate ignorance and to alleviate the grief and confusion these believers were experiencing.

So that we can better understand what is happening here, let's consider the backdrop. Paul visited the believers in Thessalonica during his second missionary journey. He had gone through Troas and Philippi. From there, he went to Thessalonica. He wasn't there for long because of great opposition. Acts 17:1-2 says that while Paul was in Thessalonica, he "reasoned [with the Jews] for three Sabbaths." So Paul was there for only a few weeks before he was forced to move on to Berea. After that, he went to Athens, then Corinth.

While in Corinth, Paul wrote to the church at Thessalonica. Evidently some of the believers had died after Paul left, and those who were still alive feared that their dead brothers and sisters in Christ would miss the rapture. In their distress, they asked Paul about what would happen to those who died before the rapture took place. Would they miss it? Would they end up being second-class citizens in eternity? Where would they fit in God's future plans for believers?

Before we look at the answers, I want to call attention to the many issues Paul addressed in 1 and 2 Thessalonians. They include election, sanctification, the Holy Spirit, mind and body and soul and spirit, the rapture, the day of the Lord, the coming man of sin, the removal of the restrainer, and much more. The manner in which Paul wrote tells us he had taught on these topics while he was in Thessalonica. He had packed a lot into a few short weeks.

Today, you can go to a church for many years and not hear all the topics Paul covered. This is especially true about Bible prophecy. There are churches that won't teach on this topic. Yet Paul made sure to teach about the rapture and the end times while he was in Thessalonica.

After Paul left, some of the Christians there already had some questions. These questions arose because Paul had been faithful to teach about the rapture. And those who teach in today's churches need to do the same. The fact Paul's instructions about the rapture are recorded for us in 1 Thessalonians 4:13-18 tells us the Lord wants all Christians to understand what this event is about.

When Paul said he didn't want the believers in Thessalonica to grieve, he wasn't saying that grieving is wrong. But we shouldn't grieve as those "who have no hope." If our deceased loved ones knew the Lord, then we have the promise of their future resurrection. There's no reason to sorrow over what might happen to them at the rapture.

In 1 Thessalonians 4:13-15, Paul used the words "asleep" and "sleep" to refer to believers who had died. The original Greek word used here is *koimeteria*, from which we get our English word *cemetery*. *Koimeteria* speaks of a sleeping place for bodies. The term has nothing to do with the soul because the soul doesn't sleep. When a believer dies, his or her soul immediately goes to be with the Lord: "To be absent from the body [is] to be present with the Lord" (2 Corinthians 5:8). And the soul of an unbeliever goes to Hades at death. In both cases, only the body falls asleep.

Many people are confused about what death really means. Death is separation from God, not the cessation of existence. Adam and Eve were warned, "In the day that you eat" of the tree of the knowledge of good and evil, "you shall surely die" (Genesis 2:17). Sure enough, at the moment they ate, they died spiritually and were immediately separated from God.

A dead person does not cease to exist. Rather, the immaterial and the material separate, with the body falling asleep, and the soul going to be with the Lord or in Hades. The material part of a person goes into the ground, and the immaterial part goes to either Christ or Hades.

When the rapture takes place, only the bodies of deceased believers will rise. Those bodies will be rejoined with their souls and spirits. But the bodies of unbelievers won't be raised until the end of Christ's 1,000-year kingdom on earth, at which time the great white throne judgment will take place. Unbelievers will then experience what is known as the second death or eternal death (Revelation 20:11-15). They will be separated from God permanently.

Going back to 1 Thessalonians 4, notice the assurance Paul gave in verse 14: "If we believe that Jesus died and rose again, even so God will bring with him those who sleep in Jesus." The Greek text here is better translated, "*Since* we believe…God will bring with Him those who sleep." Paul wasn't saying, "Maybe God will bring with Him those who sleep in Jesus." He was saying God *will* do this.

Paul then added, in verse 15, "This we say to you by the word of the Lord." This promise came to Paul by divine revelation from God. The truth about the rapture was revealed to him in 1 Corinthians 15, where this event is called "a mystery" (verse 51). In the New Testament, a mystery is a truth that has not yet been revealed and cannot be figured out by man. It can only be understood through divine revelation. And the mystery of the rapture is that a large number of people are going to do an end run on the grave. They will not experience physical death.

What did Paul say about this mystery?

> We shall not all sleep, but we shall all be changed—in a moment, in the twinkling of an eye, at the last trumpet. For the trumpet will sound, and the dead will be raised incorruptible, and we shall be changed. For this corruption must put on incorruption, and this mortal must put on immortality (1 Corinthians 15:51-53).

That's the mystery: We will not sleep. We will not die, but instead, we will be changed. At the rapture, every believer who is alive on earth will undergo a transformation and be taken up into the Lord's presence.

Before that happens, however, we are told in 1 Thessalonians 4:16 that "the dead in Christ will rise first." They will be resurrected from the grave before we are raptured. This was an enormous comfort to the believers in Thessalonica, who feared that the dead in Christ would be second-class citizens or miss the rapture. In fact, they will be taken up first!

### The Chronological Sequence of the Rapture

Next, let's look at the chronological sequence of the rapture as presented in 1 Thessalonians 4:16-17. We see four main points here: the return, the resurrection, the removal, and the reunion.

### 1. The Return

First Thessalonians 4:16 tells us how the rapture will begin: "The Lord Himself will descend from heaven with a shout, with the voice of an archangel, and with the trumpet of God."

There are very few other times in Scripture when we see Jesus shout. One was when He raised Lazarus from the dead. John 11:43 says, "He cried with a loud voice, 'Lazarus, come forth!'" The other time was when Jesus cried out from the cross, "My God, My God, why have You forsaken Me?" (Matthew 27:46). After that, He "cried out again with a loud voice, and yielded up His spirit." When that happened, the veil in the temple "was torn in two from top to bottom; and the earth quaked, and rocks were split, and the graves were opened; and many bodies of the saints who had fallen asleep were raised" (verses 50-52).

At the rapture, Jesus will give a shout from the skies—a shout that will raise dead believers and call up living believers to heaven. Accompanying this shout will be "the voice of an archangel, and with the trumpet of God" (1 Thessalonians 4:16). In Scripture, trumpets were often used to call God's people to gather together.

At the time Jesus descends with a shout, He will not come all the way to the earth. He will remain suspended in the air, and He will call up His own to Him. This is how we know the rapture is not the same as the second coming. They are two distinct events. At the rapture, Jesus will descend only partway, whereas at the second coming, He will descend all the way to earth and place His feet on the Mount of Olives (Zechariah 14:4).

As we look at the details about the rapture, we need to remember the entire event will occur in the amount of time it takes to blink your eye. First Corinthians 15:52 says it will happen "in a moment, in the twinkling of an eye." In the original Greek text, the word "moment" is *atomos*, which refers to a moment of time so short it cannot be divided any further. There are some who say "the twinkling of an eye" has to do with light reflecting off a person's eye, but it's more likely Paul was referring to the time it takes for a person to blink. We're told that "on average the human blink lasts only a tenth of a second which is 100 milliseconds."[1]

In 1 Thessalonians 4:13-17, the Lord slows down the film about the rapture so that we can see it frame by frame. But the entire event will happen in the time it takes to blink!

I have often wondered if, when the rapture happens, the people who are left here on earth will hear our Lord's shout, the voice of the archangel, and the trumpet. The Bible doesn't say. But it's interesting to note what happened to Saul when he was on the road to Damascus and the Lord stopped him in his tracks. A light shone around Saul and Jesus spoke, saying, "Saul, Saul, why are you persecuting Me?" (Acts 9:4). We're told "the men who journeyed with him stood speechless, hearing a voice but seeing no one" (verse 7). Apparently they heard sounds, but they couldn't see anything or understand what was said. We don't know for sure, but it's possible those who are left behind at the rapture will hear some kind of sound reverberating around the world. If so, that will add to the angst, drama, confusion, and fear surrounding the event.

After Jesus' return comes the next stage:

### 2. The Resurrection

First Thessalonians 4:16 says "the dead in Christ will rise first." Jesus will raise up the bodies of all deceased church-age believers. Notice that only those who are "in Christ" will be raised. This tells us the Old Testament saints won't be taken up at this time. Daniel 12:1-3 appears to confirm that, and I agree with those who say that Old Testament believers will be resurrected after the tribulation. As Daniel 12:2 says, "Many of those who sleep in the dust of the earth shall awake, some to everlasting life, some to shame and everlasting contempt."

Because the rapture involves only church-age believers, that tells us the purpose of this event is to bring an end to the church age. This era began on the day of Pentecost, when the Holy Spirit descended and came upon believers in Jerusalem (Acts 2:1-4). The church age began suddenly in a moment of time, and it will end suddenly as well.

Paul's statement that the dead in Christ will rise first was an affirmation that believers who die before the rapture won't miss it. He wanted to comfort the believers in Thessalonica, who had worried that their deceased Christian friends and family members would not be taken up in the rapture.

One question I'm often asked is whether the rapture will cause tombs and graves to be disrupted. The Bible doesn't say. There are two ways to look at this: First, remember that Jesus' resurrection body was able to pass through walls. So it's possible that when dead believers are instantaneously given their glorified bodies, they will pass right through the tomb or grave without disturbing anything. Second, when Jesus was raised from the dead, the stone in front of the tomb was rolled away. And, as we read a moment ago, when Jesus was on the cross, the tombs of many saints burst open, letting them out of the grave.

So we can't be dogmatic one way or the other—it's possible graves won't be disturbed, and it's possible they will be. If there *is* physical evidence of the resurrection after it occurs, that will have a truly eerie effect on those who are left behind. They will wonder what had happened and try to come up with explanations for it.

In the instant that the dead in Christ are raised, their bodies will be transformed. They will be brought up glorified, perfected, immortal, imperishable, and incorruptible. And their bodies will be joined back together with their perfected souls and spirits.

### 3. The Removal

After the resurrection of dead church-age believers from their graves, living believers will be removed from the earth. This is the rapture itself. Paul said, "Then we who are alive and remain shall be caught up together with them in the clouds to meet the Lord in the air" (1 Thessalonians 4:17). The words "caught up" come from the Greek word *harpazo*, which is used 13 times in the New Testament. It means "to snatch, seize, or take away suddenly," or "to transport from one place to another."

This brings us to an important point: There are many people who say the word *rapture* doesn't appear in the Bible. This is one of the arguments they use to deny the rapture. They're right when it comes to English translations of the Bible, but we have to remember the New Testament was written in Greek. When Jerome translated the Greek New Testament into Latin, he replaced *harpazo* with *rapturo*. Our English word *rapture*, which is translated "caught up" in 1 Thessalonians 4:17, comes from the Latin term *rapturo*, which traces back to the Greek word *harpazo*.

So if someone doesn't want to call this event the rapture of the church, they can call it the *harpazo*—the snatching away. Regardless of what it is called, it is going to happen. When Jesus descends from heaven with a shout, we who are alive and remain will be taken up to meet Him in the air.

To better understand the meaning of *harpazo*, let's look at the other passages where the term is used. In John 10:28, when Jesus said no one can snatch us from His hand, He used the word *harpazo*. In Acts 8:39, *harpazo* was used to describe the way God "caught Philip away" and transported him from one place to another.

In 2 Corinthians 12, Paul wrote about how he was "caught up in the third heaven" (verse 2). He was "caught up into Paradise and heard inexpressible words" that he was not permitted to speak (verse 4). I personally believe one of the reasons Paul loved the doctrine of the rapture so much is because he had experienced his own rapture. He had been caught up to the Lord, then sent back to finish his ministry.

Notice also that when Paul talked about the removal, he included himself in it. In 1 Thessalonians 4:17, he wrote, "Then *we* who are alive and remain shall be caught up." He didn't say, "Then *you*...shall be caught up." By including himself, Paul revealed his belief that the rapture could happen in his lifetime. He saw it as an imminent event that could take place at any time, and we are to live with that same sense of anticipation.

I've had people say to me, "This sounds too bizarre. Do you really believe that all of a sudden, that many people are going to disappear from the earth without dying?" While this rapture will be the largest by far, it won't be the first. God has raptured other people in the past. Enoch and Elijah were both raptured to heaven (Genesis 5:24; 2 Kings 2:1). The prophet Isaiah was caught up to God's throne room (Isaiah 6:1). When Jesus ascended to heaven, the word *harpazo* was used to indicate He was raptured (Revelation 12:5). Philip was raptured (Acts 8:39), as was Paul (2 Corinthians 12:1-4).

All those raptures were literal, historical events. They are precedents for the ultimate and final rapture—that of the church, which will also be literal and historical. Raptures have happened before, and there's another one yet to come. All the living believers on earth will be taken up, never to experience death. As one of my friends said, "I'm looking for the upper-taker, not the undertaker."

So far, we've looked at the return of Christ, the resurrection of dead believers, and the removal of living believers. That brings us to the next phase.

### 4. The Reunion

Paul wrote in 1 Thessalonians 4:17 that we will "meet the Lord in the air. And thus we shall always be with the Lord." Because the rapture will include both dead and living Christians, it will bring about an incredible reunion with all our loved ones. But the focal point of it all will be Christ Himself. He is the one who will descend, and it is those who are dead in Christ who will rise. We who are alive will be caught up to meet Him in the air, and all of us will be with Him forever. He will make the rapture happen, and it is He who made our redemption possible. It is through His power that our bodies will be changed from corruptible to incorruptible.

Have you ever thought about the fact that when we see Jesus face to face for the first time, we will not only see our Redeemer—the one who paid the price for our sins—but also the one who created us? John 1:3 says, "All things were made through Him, and without

Him nothing was made that was made." I can't imagine what it's going to be like to look at our Lord, knowing He is the one who not only redeemed me but made me. For all of us, the rapture will be an incredible first encounter with our Lord. This is not a mere *event* we are waiting for, but a *person*. We are waiting for Christ Himself to call us and take us to be with Him.

Upon reading what 1 Thessalonians 4:17 says about us being with the Lord, we can't help but wonder: Where exactly are we going?

If you happen to believe in the post-tribulation view of the rapture, which says the church will go through the entire tribulation, then your answer will be that we will go up, meet the Lord in the air, then do a quick U-turn and come right back to the earth with Him.

But if you hold to the view that the rapture will happen before the tribulation, then you will say that we are going up to meet the Lord in the air, then up again to heaven. We're going to the Father's house, as Jesus promised in John 14:1-3.

There are definite parallels between 1 Thessalonians 4:13-17 and John 14:1-3. Both passages were written to give assurance to believers. And both speak of Jesus taking us up to be with Him forever. Neither passage says anything about returning to earth right away:

> Let not your heart be troubled; you believe in God, believe
> also in Me. In My Father's house are many mansions; if
> it were not so, I would have told you. I go to prepare a
> place for you. And if I go and prepare a place for you, I
> will come again and receive you to Myself; that where I
> am, there you may be also (John 14:1-3).

After we are taken up to heaven, we will appear before the judgment seat of Christ. This judgment will be for believers only (1 Corinthians 3:12-15; 2 Corinthians 5:9-10). This judgment won't have anything to do with our salvation, for Christ has already justified us and made us righteous. Rather, this will be a judgment of rewards, a time when the Lord will examine the works we did for Him.

After that will come the marriage supper of the Lamb (Revelation 19:7-9). The church will be "arrayed in fine linen, clean and bright, for the fine linen is the righteous acts of the saints." Both the judgment seat of Christ and the marriage supper will take place in heaven while the tribulation unfolds on the earth.

Paul then concluded 1 Thessalonians 4:13-18, saying, "Therefore comfort one another with these words" (verse 18). The doctrine of the rapture is meant to comfort us and give us hope. This is true in every place where it is mentioned in the Bible. The promise of the rapture fills us with hope because it means we will see our deceased loved ones and friends again. It means that we're not saying good-bye forever; we will see one another again. We can find great assurance in the truths that we *will* be taken up, we *will* be reunited, and we *will* be with our Lord forever.

## WHEN WILL THE RAPTURE TAKE PLACE?

Now let's look at the timing of the rapture. By that I don't mean the day and hour, but rather, where the rapture lands on God's chronological time line for the last days. There are five main views:

- pre-tribulation rapture

- partial rapture

- mid-tribulation rapture

- post-tribulation rapture

- pre-wrath rapture

We'll look briefly at each view, then I will explain the reasons I believe the pre-trib rapture lines up with Scripture the best. This is important because lately, many people have attacked the pre-trib view. Unfortunately, many of them don't understand it in the first place.

One of their criticisms is that if you believe in the pre-trib rapture, you believe in two second comings. But that is not correct. In the rapture, we will be taken up to meet Christ in the air, then go to heaven. Jesus won't come back to earth until the end of the tribulation. The pre-trib view says there is one coming, but it will occur in two phases. In the first phase, Jesus will come *for* His saints, and in the second phase, He will come *with* His saints. In the first phase, all of us will go to heaven and stay there. Not until the second phase will Christ come back to the earth.

Another common argument against the pre-trib view is people claim it is relatively new. They say it was invented in the 1830s by J.N. Darby. But that's not correct. The historical antecedent for the rapture goes all the way back to the early church fathers. You'll find this evidence documented in a book I published with Dr. Ed Hindson, titled *Can We Still Believe in the Rapture?*[2] One example of a pre-trib proponent who predates J.N. Darby is Morgan Edwards, who founded what is now known as Brown University. He held to a pre-trib rapture view back in the 1740s, nearly 100 years before Darby.

As I address these criticisms, I want to say that the whole matter of the timing of the rapture makes for legitimate discussion between Christians. Our view of the timing of the rapture is not a test of fellowship or of a person's salvation. But if we're going to debate the merits of the different views, we should represent them accurately. The two criticisms I've shared above—about two second comings and about J.N. Darby—are straw-man arguments. They are not accurate, and therefore are not legitimate points of debate.

### The Partial-Rapture View

The proponents of this view say that at the rapture, only faithful, dedicated Christians will be caught up. They believe that carnal

Christians will be left behind to be chastened during the tribulation period. What's interesting is that every person I've met who advocates this view believes they will be part of the first group of believers raptured to heaven. I've never met anyone who thinks they will be taken up later on.

There are some who believe there will be several raptures during the tribulation. As people become ready, they will be caught up at different times.

One of the key problems with the partial rapture theory is that according to 1 Thessalonians 4:16-17, the only qualification for being caught up is that we have to be in Christ. If Paul said that "the dead in Christ will rise first," we have to assume that all who are alive and "in Christ" will be taken up. There aren't different degrees of being in Christ. Either you are in Christ, or you aren't. Either you're a believer, or you're not.

In 1 Corinthians 15:51, we read, "We shall not all sleep, but we shall all be changed." When the rapture happens, *all* of us will take part. Paul didn't say some will be raptured and others won't.

Also, it doesn't make sense for the body of Christ to be divided, with part of it going to heaven and part of it staying on earth. We are all the body of Christ.

### The Mid-Trib Rapture View

This view says the rapture will occur at the middle of the tribulation. This means believers will have to endure the first half. Those who hold the mid-trib view also say believers are not appointed to God's wrath. They believe that the first half of this seven-year period will be relatively peaceful, and that the outpouring of God's wrath will take place during the last half of the tribulation.

The difficulty with this view is that according to Revelation chapter 6, the first seal judgments will occur at the beginning of the tribulation. These initial judgments include the four horsemen of the apocalypse, through which God will express His wrath against those who are on the earth. Jesus is the one who will open the seven seals, with the first one opened in Revelation 6:1—right at the start.

While it is true that the tribulation will get worse as time goes on, still, the fact the seven seals are opened at the beginning tells us God's wrath will be expressed during all seven years.

The mid-trib view also prevents any possibility that the rapture is imminent. If the mid-trib view is correct, then it would be possible to calculate when the rapture will happen. The mid-trib view requires that three-and-a-half years of the tribulation go by before the rapture occurs. But that is at odds with what Jesus said about not knowing the day or the hour.

### The Post-Trib Rapture View

This view says the rapture will happen at the end of the tribulation, which means believers will have to endure all seven years of God's wrath upon the earth.

But if we should expect to endure the tribulation, why doesn't the New Testament tell us how to prepare? Have you ever noticed there are no instructions for what Christians are to do during that seven-year period of wrath? I believe the reason we're not given any guidance is because we won't be here.

Consider this: Two days before He was crucified, Jesus said, "When the Son of Man comes in His glory, and all the holy angels with Him, then He will sit on the throne of His glory. All the nations will be gathered before Him, and He will separate them one from another, as a shepherd divides his sheep from the goats" (Matthew 25:31-32). At the second coming, Jesus will separate the sheep from the goats—the believers from the unbelievers.

This raises a question: If the rapture is at the end of the tribulation, and the sheep are caught up to heaven then make a U-turn and come right back to earth, who will be left on earth? Only the goats. There won't be any sheep because they will have already been taken up.

For Jesus to say He will separate the sheep from the goats while they are still on earth tells us the rapture isn't at the end of the tribulation. It makes more sense for the rapture to occur at the beginning. Then those who become Christians during the tribulation will be the sheep who are separated from the goats at the end of the seven-year period.

Another problem with the post-trib view is that it makes the rapture inconsequential. If believers have already gone all the way through the tribulation, why have a rapture? Why have Christians go up to heaven only to return immediately to earth? Why not let believers wait for Jesus to come to earth? The post-trib view makes the rapture anticlimactic.

The post-trib view also denies the imminency of the rapture. Again, we're not supposed to know when the rapture will happen. But if it's at the end of the tribulation, the timing can be calculated.

### The Pre-Wrath Rapture View

This view has gained somewhat of a following in recent decades. It advocates the rapture will take place not at the middle or the end of the tribulation, but roughly three-quarters of the way through. This view states that God's wrath won't really start up until sometime during the second half of the tribulation.

But the Lamb—the Lord Jesus Christ—will begin opening the seal judgments at the beginning of the tribulation, according to Revelation 6. This means the entire seven-year period will be a time of wrath, and the wrath will escalate as time goes on. The pre-wrath view also diminishes any possibility that the rapture could be imminent. It doesn't allow for Jesus to come back at any moment of time.

### The Pre-Trib Rapture View

This view says the rapture will occur before the tribulation and will include all believers in Jesus Christ. Here are among the reasons I hold to this view:

*1. There is no mention of the church from Revelation chapters 4 through 19.* The word "church," which is the Greek term *ekklesia*, appears 19 times in Revelation chapters 1 through 3, and again in Revelation 22:16. In between, during the tribulation, the church is never mentioned. That tells us the church will be absent during the tribulation. We won't be here on earth.

*2. The New Testament tells us believers will be exempt from divine wrath.* First Thessalonians 1:10 talks about how we, as believers, "wait for His Son from heaven…even Jesus who delivers us from the wrath to come." We are waiting for our Lord to take us up before the tribulation starts.

First Thessalonians 5:9 says, "God did not appoint us to wrath, but to obtain salvation through our Lord Jesus Christ." This isn't talking about the wrath of hell, but the wrath that will come during the day of the Lord, or the tribulation. That is the context of 1 Thessalonians 5:1-11.

In Revelation 3:10, the Lord says, "I…will keep you from the hour of trial which shall come upon the whole world, to test those who dwell on the earth." Notice Jesus didn't say, "I'm going to deliver you from the testing." He said, "I'm going to deliver you from the *hour* of trial"—from the *time* of testing. We won't be here during that time.

Here is an illustration that depicts the difference between the pre-trib and post-trib views: Imagine you're part of a large class that I teach. At the end of the semester, I say, "If you already have an *A* in the class, you still have to show up for the time of the final exam, but you don't have to take it." That's the post-trib view—you have to be present while the test is taken. But suppose I say, "If you already have an *A* in the class, you don't have to show up for the test. You are exempt from that hour." That's the pre-trib view, and that's what the Lord says in Revelation 3:10: "I…will keep you from the hour of trial."

*3. Believers won't experience the same things unbelievers will.* Read 1 Thessalonians 5:1-4 on page 74, and note carefully how the pronouns shift. I have italicized them so you can see what happens:

> Concerning the times and the seasons, brethren, *you* have no need that I should write to *you*. For *you yourselves* know perfectly that the day of the Lord so comes as a thief in the night. For when *they* say, "Peace and safety!" then sudden destruction comes upon *them*, as labor pains upon a pregnant woman. And *they* shall not escape. But *you*, brethren, are not in darkness, so that this Day should overtake *you* as a thief.

Did you notice how the passage first talks about believers (you), then unbelievers (they), then believers again (you)? There's a sharp contrast here. It's not the believers who will say, "Peace and safety!" but unbelievers. It's not believers who won't be able to escape, but unbelievers. The pronouns make clear distinctions here. Believers won't experience the same things unbelievers will. Why? Because they will not be present on the earth during the tribulation.

4. *Only a pre-trib rapture can give us comfort, not a post-trib rapture.* Still another passage in support of the pre-trib view is 1 Thessalonians 4:18. After Paul described what will happen during the rapture, he wrote, "Comfort one another with these words." How comforting would it be if Christians were told they had to go through the entire tribulation? That wouldn't be comforting at all.

Titus 2:13 describes the rapture as "the blessed hope." Tim LaHaye used to say that if believers were required to go through the tribulation, then the rapture wouldn't be a blessed hope, but a blasted hope. It would be better to die before the tribulation, wouldn't it? But the reason the doctrine of the rapture is a comfort is because we won't be here on earth to face God's wrath.

5. *The sequence of the events written in 1 Thessalonians 4–5.* Notice the sequence of Paul's presentation in 1 Thessalonians chapters 4 and 5. First, in 4:13-18, he talked about the rapture. Then he explained the day of the Lord, or the tribulation, in 5:1-6. The rapture was mentioned first, then the day of the Lord.

*6. The doctrine of imminency.* Still another point in favor of the pre-trib view is the doctrine of imminency. This doesn't mean the rapture must happen soon. Rather, it means there is nothing that needs to happen before the rapture can occur. It is a sign-less event. It will occur, but we don't know when. That's what is meant by imminency.

Notice that in 1 Corinthians 16:22, Paul wrote, "O Lord, come!" The Aramaic word there is *maranatha*, and this is the only time it appears in the New Testament. *Maranatha* means "Our Lord come." But if He cannot come at any time, why say, "Maranatha"? If the mid-trib or post-trib views were correct, the Lord wouldn't be able to come back for at least three-and-a-half years, or seven years. The pre-wrath rapture view has the same problem.

The early church lived with the expectancy that Christ could come at any time. Only in that context does it make sense to say, "Maranatha." Because it was an Aramaic word, Christians could say it to one another without very many Greek-speaking people knowing what they meant.

There are other passages that communicate imminency. In Philippians 3:20, Paul wrote, "Our citizenship is in heaven, from which we also eagerly wait for the Savior, the Lord Jesus Christ." We are to eagerly await Him; there is no expectation of anything that must happen before we are snatched up. First Thessalonians 1:10 says we are "to wait for His Son from heaven." Titus 2:13 urges us to be "looking for the blessed hope and glorious appearing of our great God and Savior Jesus Christ." Paul didn't say we're to watch for the antichrist or the tribulation.

If you hold to the mid-trib, pre-wrath rapture, or post-trib views, as well as the partial rapture view, you cannot legitimately say Jesus could come back at any moment. Instead, Jesus will come back either three-and-a-half years, or five years, or seven years, or at some point during the tribulation. None of those views allow for imminency.

The beauty of the doctrine of imminency is that it changes the way we live. The possibility Jesus could rapture us today affects what we do and don't do. It has a powerful and motivating influence on us. The knowledge that we must always be ready has a purifying effect on us. When we fail to uphold the truth that Christ could come at any moment, we no longer live with a sense of urgency. We become careless about how we live—we become less committed and less motivated to holiness and godliness.

Dr. John Walvoord, who studied Bible prophecy carefully, came up with 50 reasons that the pre-trib rapture view made sense.[3] I don't have the space to list them here, but we've gone through several key reasons above.

## ARE YOU READY FOR THE RAPTURE?

If you're not in Christ when the rapture happens, you won't be ready. You will be left behind. In the well-loved song "Rock of Ages" are some words that beautifully present the truth of salvation:

> Could my zeal no respite know,
> Could my tears forever flow,
> All could never sin erase,
> Thou must save, and save by grace.
>
> Nothing in my hands I bring,
> Simply to Thy cross I cling.[4]

To become saved, we must come to Christ with empty hands. There is nothing we can offer to Him to merit or earn our salvation. All we can cling to is the cross of Christ. We must place our trust wholly in Him and cast ourselves completely upon Him to be our Savior.

If you have never trusted Christ as your Lord and Savior, I urge you to pray to Him and say, "Lord, I come to You right now with nothing of my own merit or works. I come and cling to Jesus Christ and Him alone as my Rock of ages, as my Savior."

And if you are already a Christian, you need to be prepared. You need to live your life for the Lord Jesus as if He could come at any time. It is the Lord Himself who will descend, and we will be caught up in the air to be with Him forever. We are to look forward to that day when our faith will become sight, when we will look face to face at our Redeemer and Creator. As we live in light of that day, we will be filled with hope.

# CHAPTER 5

# WHAT YOU BELIEVE ABOUT THE RAPTURE AND WHY IT MATTERS

## JACK HIBBS

The rapture is clearly taught in the Bible, yet there are people who say, "No, it's not." Scripture warns us that "scoffers will come in the last days...saying, 'Where is the promise of His coming?'" (2 Peter 3:3). The apostle Paul said that "in the last days...evil men and impostors will grow worse and worse, deceiving and being deceived" (2 Timothy 3:1, 13). We need to be careful that we're not misled by persuasive arguments, or swayed by a person's name or stature. Instead, we need to examine the fruit of their life. Are they living out the truth? Are they proclaiming the gospel correctly? That's what we need to pay attention to.

That's the reason I've titled this message "What You Believe About the Rapture and Why It Matters." The doctrine of the rapture appears in the Bible, and your view of the rapture will affect how you live. Are you living in response to that truth?

## OUR VIEW OF THE RAPTURE

At the end of my emails and letters, I always sign off with "Awaiting His return." That expresses how we're to live—in anticipation of Christ's coming. Titus 2:13 says we're to be "looking for the blessed hope and glorious appearing of our great God and Savior Jesus Christ." We're to wait with eager hearts. That's how the doctrine of the rapture should affect us.

Some people say, "What if Jesus doesn't come back for another 10 years, or even 50 years?" That doesn't matter. We are commanded to occupy till He comes (Luke 19:13). We're to stay busy doing His work, yet we're also to be ready for the possibility He could come at any moment.

Colossians 3:1-4 sums up beautifully the perspective and mindset we should have as Christians who await the rapture:

> If then you were raised with Christ, seek those things which are above, where Christ is, sitting at the right hand of God. Set your mind on things above, not on things on the earth. For you died, and your life is hidden with Christ in God. When Christ who is our life appears, then you also will appear with Him in glory.

As those who were raised with Christ, we are to seek the things that are above, not what is cool or trending. We're to set our minds on what is of God, and not of earth. We're to be ready for Christ's appearance. And when He comes to rapture us, we will appear with Him in glory.

## WHY THE RAPTURE MATTERS

### Because the Rapture Is a Biblical Doctrine

The first reason the rapture should matters to us is because it is a biblical doctrine. While the English word *rapture* doesn't appear in Scripture, it does appear in the Latin Bible as the term *rapturo*. It means "to be caught up, to be pulled up suddenly." It speaks of being taken from one place to another, as happened with Philip in Acts 8. There, we see Philip ministering to "a man of Ethiopia" and helping him to understand the Scriptures (verse 27). After the man received Christ as Savior and was baptized, the Holy Spirit "caught Philip away" and transported him to Azotus (verse 39). That was a rapture.

The prophet Elijah was raptured as well. "Suddenly a chariot of fire appeared with horses of fire...and Elijah went up by a whirlwind into heaven" (2 Kings 2:11). He was taken up to heaven without ever facing death.

Enoch, who was the father of Methuselah and lived before the flood, was also raptured: "By faith Enoch was taken away so that he did not see death, 'and was not found, because God had taken him'" (Hebrews 11:5).

The Lord Jesus Christ introduced the doctrine of the rapture in John 14:1-3. Here's what He said:

> Let not your heart be troubled; you believe in God, believe also in Me. In My Father's house are many mansions; if it were not so, I would have told you. I go to prepare a place for you. And if I go and prepare a place for you, I will come again and receive you to Myself; that where I am, there you may be also.

Jesus will take us up to the Father's house (singular), which has many mansions (plural). This will be one house with many places. Jesus went there after He ascended to heaven in Acts 1:9, and He has been working on our dwelling places ever since. They will be glorious!

Jesus' promise "I will come again and receive you to Myself" lines up with what we read a moment ago from Colossians 3:4: "When Christ who is our life appears, then you also will appear with Him in glory."

### An Undeniable Truth

If you don't believe in the rapture, then you'll have to get a pair of scissors and cut John 14:1-3 out of your Bible. Notice that I'm *not* talking about the timing of the rapture—about whether we will be taken up before, during, or after the tribulation. We can debate the timing. But the rapture itself is clearly taught in Scripture. We see people taken up to heaven or from one place to another. And Jesus taught about the rapture, as well as the apostle Paul.

In fact, it's interesting to note that Paul ministered to the church in Thessalonica for only three or four weeks. During that short span of time, he taught the essential doctrines of the faith to them—including the doctrine of the rapture. How do we know this? In 1 Thessalonians 4, Paul comforted those who were distressed because they feared that believers who had already died would miss the rapture (verses 13-17). The only way these church members could have been worried is if they were expecting the rapture to happen. Paul must have taught them about this event during his short time in Thessalonica. That tells us Paul had made a priority of teaching them about the rapture.

Today, the doctrine of the rapture is more important than ever. Some of us may differ on the timing, but we cannot say, "There is no rapture." It's clearly taught in Scripture. Pastors need to teach about it, and all believers should know about it. God gave us the promise of the rapture because it is meant to fill us with hope. He wants us to anticipate this wonderful event.

There are some who say we shouldn't talk about the rapture because it'll make us so heavenly minded that we are no earthly good. But the opposite is true. It's when we are heavenly minded that we are spurred to do more earthly good!

### A Repeated Truth

How important is the doctrine of the rapture? Paul wrote about it in all five chapters of 1 Thessalonians:

1. 1 THESSALONIANS 1:10

> ...to wait for His Son from heaven, whom He raised from
> the dead, even Jesus who delivers us from the wrath to come.

Here, the word "wrath" refers to God's anger and judgment. It has nothing to do with hell. Rather, this speaks about the future day when God will pour out His wrath upon the people on earth. This passage promises we will be delivered from that wrath—that is, raptured to heaven. That's because God's wrath is meant for a Christ-rejecting world, not us.

2. 1 THESSALONIANS 2:19

> What is our hope, or joy, or crown of rejoicing? Is it not even
> you in the presence of the Lord Jesus Christ at His coming?

Jesus will return to take us up in the rapture. We can be sure of that.

3. 1 THESSALONIANS 3:13

> ...so that He may establish your hearts blameless in holiness
> before our God and Father at the coming of our Lord
> Jesus Christ with all His saints.

Once again, Paul talks about the promise of the rapture. As he does so, he calls believers "saints." This is true of all the believers who are now in heaven, and it's true about those of us who are still here on earth. We are saints not because of our own goodness, but because we have been made righteous in Christ.

4. 1 THESSALONIANS 4:14

> If we believe that Jesus died and rose again, even so also
> God will bring with Him those who sleep in Jesus.

"Sleep" was an affectionate term used by the early church to refer to believers who had died. We can also apply this idea of "sleep" to the Old Testament saints. God told David, "When your days are fulfilled and you rest with your fathers, I will set up your seed after you" (2 Samuel 7:12). In this case, "rest" means "sleep." This term was used only in connection with the death of a body. It was never used to speak of the soul, which goes immediately into Jesus' presence when a person dies.

When Paul taught about the rapture, he said, "We who are alive and remain until the coming of the Lord will by no means precede those who are asleep" (1 Thessalonians 4:15). Those who have died and whose bodies are in the ground will rise first. "Then we who are alive and remain shall be caught up" (verse 17). "Caught up" is translated from the Greek word *harpazo*, which was translated *rapturo* in the Latin Bible. That's where we get our English word *rapture*. And where will we be caught up to? "In the clouds to meet the Lord in the air" (verse 17).

Again, this takes us back to what we read in Colossians 3:4: "When Christ who is our life appears, then you also will appear with Him in glory."

## 5. 1 Thessalonians 5:9

> God did not appoint us to wrath, but to obtain salvation through our Lord Jesus Christ.

God will deliver us from the wrath to come. We will not face the seven-year tribulation, when God judges the whole earth. One of God's purposes for this time period is to draw the people of Israel to Him. This is a time meant not only to judge the world, but to get the attention of the Jews. That is made clear in Daniel 9:24, where the angel Gabriel tells Daniel, "Seventy weeks are determined for your people and for your holy city." This seventy-weeks period includes a final week that is the seven-year tribulation, a time meant for Daniel's people and their holy city—that is, the Jews and Jerusalem.

Another reason we know the church won't be on earth during the rapture is because of what happens in Revelation 4:1. In Revelation chapters 2–3, Jesus speaks to the church through the apostle John. But then John is taken up to heaven in Revelation 4:1. From that point all the way to Revelation 18, we do not see the church evident anywhere on earth. You'll also notice the book of Revelation doesn't instruct us about survival tactics during the tribulation. That's because we won't be here.

Not until Revelation 19—when Jesus descends from heaven followed by the church riding on white horses—do we see the church again. All of us will be "clothed in fine linen, white and clean" (verse 14). We, the bride of Christ, will be His army. We read that "out of [Christ's] mouth goes a sharp sword, that with it He should strike the nations" (verse 15).

The only way it would be possible for us to follow Christ from heaven to earth is if we had been raptured to heaven prior to the tribulation.

### The Remarkable Parallels

One reason we know both Jesus and Paul were talking about the rapture in John 14 and 1 Thessalonians 4 is because the two passages line up with each other. Here are the parallels:

- In John 14, Jesus began, "Let not your heart be troubled" (verse 1). In 1 Thessalonians 4, Paul told the church not to grieve for believers who had "fallen asleep" (verse 13).

- Jesus talked about "My Father" (John 14:2), and Paul spoke of Jesus and God the Father (1 Thessalonians 4:14).

- Jesus said, "I...have told you" (John 14:2), and Paul wrote, "We say to you by the word of the Lord" (1 Thessalonians 4:15).

- Jesus said, "I will come again" (John 14:3), and Paul described "the coming of the Lord" (1 Thessalonians 4:15).

- Jesus said, "[I will] receive you to Myself" (John 14:3), and Paul explained, "We...shall be caught up together" (1 Thessalonians 4:17).

- Jesus spoke of taking us up to Himself (John 14:3), and Paul said we will "meet the Lord in the air" (1 Thessalonians 4:17).

- Finally, Jesus stated the end result of the rapture: "that where I am, there you may be also" (John 14:3). Likewise, Paul said, "We shall always be with the Lord" (1 Thessalonians 4:17).

The two passages are clearly talking about the same event.

### Because the Rapture Is Our Hope

The doctrine of the rapture is meant to encourage us, not to stir up arguments or division. As Titus 2:13 says, we are to be "looking for the blessed hope and glorious appearing of our great God and Savior Jesus Christ." For all believers in every age, the rapture always has been and always will be the blessed hope that we look forward to. That's because we know God will fulfill His Word. He will keep His promise!

Paul himself anticipated the rapture. That didn't change until it became obvious to him that he would soon die. He is in prison in Rome, and in 2 Timothy 4, we read his last words, which are deeply moving. He wrote, "I am already being poured out as a drink offering, and the time of my departure is at hand. I have fought the good fight, I have finished the race, I have kept the faith" (verses 6-7).

Paul was ready to depart. The fight was over. He was done running the race. He had completed the work God had called him to do. We should all want to be able to say these words when we reach the end of our life. "I have fought the good fight" is on my father-in-law's tombstone. Is this your heart's desire as well?

Paul then said, "There is laid up for me a crown of righteousness, which the Lord, the righteous Judge, will give to me on that Day, and not to me only but also to all who have loved His appearing" (2 Timothy 4:8). It wasn't until shortly before his death that Paul spoke of loving Christ's appearing in the *past* tense. Up till then, he was always looking forward to the rapture, saying, "We who are alive and remain shall be caught up together with them" (1 Thessalonians 4:17).

This tells us that if we end up not being raptured, we have nothing to worry about. Jesus will be holding our hand at the moment of death. He will not abandon us—He will be with us forever. As Paul wrote, "To be absent from the body [is] to be present with the Lord" (2 Corinthians 5:8). Whether we are raptured or not, we will be with Jesus. What a blessed hope we have!

### Because the Rapture Is the Great Motivator

In a parable, Jesus taught, "Do business till I come" (Luke 19:13). The King James Version words this "Occupy till I come." The fact Christ could take us up to Himself at any time should motivate us to stay active for Him. I believe that all through church history, those who have expected that Jesus could come at any time are the ones who have had the greatest impact on this world. We are to stay actively engaged so we can have a positive effect on those around us. That's our calling.

Wherever God has placed you, stay busy for Him. You'll also want to look for opportunities to have an influence on others. That may mean running for office. Or joining a school board. Or getting involved with a cause or organization. You may think, *Aren't Christians supposed to avoid politics?* We see government and politics in the Bible. David was a king. The prophets spoke to kings and other leaders. Paul invoked his rights as a Roman citizen when he was arrested and put on trial. In Romans 13:1-7, we're called to be good citizens and subject to governing authorities for a reason: so that our lives may shine God's light to others. We're to be active for the sake of the truth.

The fact Christ could return at any time should motivate us to use our time well. And as long as Jesus doesn't return, we should do all we can to have a positive influence on this messed-up world.

One of the most important ways you can occupy till Jesus comes is to stay active in a church. Here's a scriptural command meant to motivate us, and it has the rapture in mind: "Let us consider one another in order to stir up love and good works, not forsaking the assembling of ourselves together, as is the manner of some, but exhorting one another, and so much more as you see the Day approaching" (Hebrews 10:24-25).

We shouldn't stop gathering with fellow believers. We're to build up and encourage one another as we "see the Day approaching." Participating in church life is vital.

### Because the Rapture Spurs Us to Personal Purity

First John 3:2-3 says, "Beloved, now we are children of God; and it has not yet been revealed what we shall be, but we know that when He is revealed, we shall be like Him, for we shall see Him as He is. And everyone who thus hopes in Him purifies himself as He is pure." What does the person who awaits the rapture do? He "purifies himself."

Jesus is coming back. And it is important that we remember the great sacrifice He made on our behalf. Hebrews 9:28 says, "Christ was offered once to bear the sins of many." He bore our sins so we could be forgiven. Isn't that incredible? Then the passage goes on to say, "To those who eagerly wait for Him He will appear a second time, apart from sin, for salvation."

Are you eagerly waiting for Jesus? Does the thought that He could come today excite you? When you find yourself backsliding or losing your excitement, love should keep you going. It should keep you motivated. Make sure you pray, "Lord, cause my heart to love You more every day. Don't let my love grow cold. May it always burn hotter for You."

You should also be motivated by the fear that Jesus could come back at a time when you're doing something you shouldn't be. Ultimately, the knowledge that the rapture could happen at any time should spur you to purity.

### Because the Rapture Is the Great Separator

Through the rapture, God will separate His people from a Christ-rejecting world before the tribulation begins. In the books of Isaiah and Revelation, unbelievers are called "dwellers on the earth" (Isaiah 18:3) and "those who dwell on the earth" (Revelation 3:10; 6:10; 11:10; 13:14; 14:6; 17:8). These earth dwellers are destined for God's wrath, not those who belong to the church. It is those who shake their fists at God and refuse to repent who will hide themselves "in the caves and the rocks of the mountains" to shelter themselves from God's wrath (Revelation 6:15). It's hard to imagine, but they will refuse to believe.

Speaking of the great separation, Paul wrote, "We shall all be changed—in a moment, in the twinkling of an eye" (1 Corinthians 15:51-52). That ought to excite you! Galatians 5:5 says, "We through the Spirit eagerly wait for the hope of righteousness by faith." That's a reference to Jesus' coming, for which we should "eagerly wait."

### Because the Rapture Will Deliver Us from God's Wrath

There are some who say those of us who teach the rapture are advocating escapism. They accuse us of wanting to deny the tribulation or evade it. But look at what Jesus Himself said:

> Let your waist be girded and your lamps burning; and you yourselves be like men who wait for their master...Blessed are those servants whom the master, when he comes, will find watching...Therefore you also be ready, for the Son of Man is coming at an hour you do not expect (Luke 12:35, 37, 40).

Why should we be waiting and ready? Luke 21:36 has the answer: "Watch therefore, and pray always that you may be counted worthy to escape all these things that will come to pass." Did you catch that word "escape"? There is no reason for us to apologize for wanting to leave the earth before the tribulation. It's not because we are cowards, but because God has promised to spare us from the wrath He will pour out.

### Because the Rapture Is Part of God's Plan for the Church

God's purpose for the rapture is to remove His people from earth before the tribulation begins.

The rapture is not for the Old Testament saints or the tribulation saints. It's solely for the bride of Christ. In John 14:1-3, Jesus gave the promise of the rapture to His disciples, who helped to begin the church. And in 1 Thessalonians 4:13-18, Paul taught about the rapture to the church. In Revelation 4:1, when John was taken up to heaven before the tribulation began, he represented the church being taken up to heaven prior to that seven-year period of wrath. John wrote, "After these things I looked, and behold, a door standing open in heaven. And the first voice which I heard was like a trumpet speaking with me, saying, 'Come up here, and I will show you things which must take place after this.'"

From Revelation 4:1 onward, God revealed to John what would happen during the tribulation. Nowhere do we see the church mentioned—not until Revelation 19, when the church will return from heaven with Christ. This affirms that the rapture is for the church.

### Because the Rapture Demonstrates God's Mercy

God will remove us before He punishes the people of the world for their sins. There is no reason for us to face God's wrath. Christ has already done that for us on the cross. Notice what Romans 5:8-9 says: "God demonstrates His own love toward us, in that while we were still sinners, Christ died for us. Much more then, having now been justified by His blood, we shall be saved from wrath through Him."

Did you catch that? We will be "saved from wrath." Later, in Romans 8:1, we read, "There is therefore now no condemnation to those who are in Christ Jesus." No condemnation!

Through the rapture, God shows His mercy to us. As 1 Thessalonians 5:9 says, "God did not appoint us to wrath."

### Because the Rapture Is in the Believer's DNA

I believe the doctrines of the rapture and of Christ's imminent return are imprinted upon us by the Holy Spirit, and therefore, are part of our spiritual DNA. I cannot imagine a Christian reading the Bible and saying, "I hope the Lord doesn't come soon." That doesn't make sense. As those who belong to Christ, we should eagerly *want* to be with Him. And we should *want* the world to be restored to righteousness. A love for the rapture should be a natural part of us.

### Because the Rapture Teaches Us to Expect Christ

In Daniel 9:24-27, God revealed to the Jewish people an outline for the coming of the Messiah. It is here that we read what will happen to Jesus here on earth. Verse 24 opens by telling us this outline covers a time span of "seventy weeks." When we calculate the numbers in the context of the passage, we realize this is talking about 70 weeks of 7 years, or 490 years.

Verses 25-26 then tell us that after "seven weeks and sixty two weeks"—which comes to 69 weeks of 7 years, or 483 years—"Messiah shall be cut off." The Messiah would come to the people of Israel, then He would die.

This countdown was to begin "from the going forth of the command to restore and build Jerusalem" (verse 25). If we start at that point of this command and count all the way to when Jesus entered Jerusalem on Palm Sunday, we come to exactly 483 years. Do you remember what Jesus said to the people in Jerusalem that week?

> O Jerusalem, Jerusalem, the one who kills the prophets and stones those who are sent to her! How often I wanted to gather your children together, as a hen gathers her chicks under her wings, but you were not willing! See! Your house is left to you desolate; for I say to you, you shall see Me no more till you say, "Blessed is He who comes in the name of the LORD!" (Matthew 23:37-39).

Jesus was rejected and crucified. This happened in year 483 of a 490-year prophecy. Jesus then warned that because the people "did not know the time of your visitation" (Luke 19:44), judgment would come.

In year 483 of Daniel's prophecy, the prophetic time clock stopped. There is still one more stretch of 7 years to go, and that will be the tribulation period. During the tribulation, God will work in the hearts of His people, drawing them to Him (Zechariah 12:10-12).

Daniel teaches we're to expect the first and second comings of Christ. And the rapture will occur before His second coming. We will be taken up to meet Jesus in the air, which is why this event is called "the blessed hope" (Titus 2:13). The truth about the rapture is to fill us with expectancy.

## A SURE AND BLESSED HOPE

We believe in the rapture not simply because we want it to happen, but because it is clearly taught in Scripture. Jesus, Paul, and John all affirmed a coming rapture. It has several purposes, all of which are important and should excite us. This makes it clear the rapture is no small matter. Rather, it is an important truth.

God promises the rapture will take place, and we know He keeps His promises. We are commanded to watch for the rapture and to live in anticipation of it because of all that it means to us. No wonder it is called the blessed hope!

CHAPTER 6

# WHY WE CAN STILL BELIEVE IN A RAPTURE

### ED HINDSON

**M**ore and more these days, we are hearing people ask the question, "Can we still believe in the rapture?" And we are seeing a number of pastors, churches, and ministries that at one time affirmed belief in the rapture are now moving away from it.

I'm convinced that sometimes it's because pastors are not willing to do the hard work of studying what the Bible really says about the future. Other times, I think people are reacting to overstatements that have been made by those who intend to defend the idea of a rapture, and in doing so, have overspeculated on the details.

The facts of Bible prophecy are very clear and always have been. After Judas left the upper room during the Last Supper, Jesus told the 11 remaining disciples, "If I go and prepare a place for you, I will come again and receive you to Myself" (John 14:3). The promise of the return of Christ is clear in God's Word.

Every legitimate Christian denomination on the planet has a statement somewhere in their statement of faith affirming the second coming of Christ. It is part of the doctrine of the Catholic Church, the

Presbyterian Church, the Westminster Convention, the Augsburg Confession of the Lutheran Church, the Baptist faith and message statement, and the list goes on. Even a theologian as liberal as Emil Brunner once said, "A Christian faith without expectation of the *Parousia* [second coming] is like a ladder which leads nowhere but ends in the void."[1] Every Christian believes that one day, Jesus will return. The simple questions are *When?* and *How?*

There are many passages in the Bible that talk about the rapture. Jesus introduces the concept of the rapture in the upper room in John 14—He is going back to heaven, and He will return to take us to the Father's house. We also see the apostle Paul explain the rapture in 1 Thessalonians 4:13-18. For the rest of this chapter, this will be our scripture of focus.

It is important to understand who wrote 1 Thessalonians, to whom it was written, and when. The writer was Paul himself. On his second missionary journey, he went into Macedonia and made his way to the town of Thessalonica. The city is still present in northern Greece today. Paul stayed three weeks, preached the gospel, planted the church, and taught Christian doctrine—including the doctrine of the second coming of Christ. After Paul departed, he wrote a letter to the church within only a few months—the letter of 1 Thessalonians.

Most scholars date 1 Thessalonians to around AD 51, less than 20 years after Jesus went to the cross and rose again. Paul was already out preaching the gospel and teaching people about the doctrine of the second coming. But during the months he was away from Thessalonica, some of the believers within the church had passed away, and those who remained became concerned. They asked, "Does this mean they will miss the rapture?" First Thessalonians 4:13-18 is Paul's response to that question:

> I do not want you to be ignorant, brethren, concerning those who have fallen asleep, lest you sorrow as others who

have no hope. For if we believe that Jesus died and rose again, even so God will bring with Him those who sleep in Jesus. For this we say to you by the word of the Lord, that we who are alive and remain until the coming of the Lord will by no means precede those who are asleep. For the Lord Himself will descend from heaven with a shout, with the voice of an archangel, and with the trumpet of God. And the dead in Christ will rise first. Then we who are alive and remain shall be caught up together with them in the clouds to meet the Lord in the air. And thus we shall always be with the Lord. Therefore comfort one another with these words.

Here's what Paul wanted the believers in Thessalonica to know: "The dead in Christ will rise first. Then we who are alive and remain *shall be caught up*" (verses 16-17). That refers to the rapture! There will come a time when the dead are raised, and then the living will be caught up to the clouds to meet the Lord in the air. Those who had died in Christ would not miss the rapture.

## SEVEN ASSURANCES OF THE RAPTURE

On one occasion, I was in a church listening to a pastor who happens to be a friend of mine. He didn't believe in a rapture per se—at least not a pre-tribulational rapture. He preached an entire sermon against the rapture, and at the end, he said, "So you see, there will never be a rapture. All we have to look forward to is trouble, trouble, and more trouble." And the audience in his church groaned out loud.

I wanted to stand up and shout, "Therefore comfort one another with these words!" But I didn't. After the service, I talked to him personally and said, "You and I both know there has to be a rapture. You just don't believe it will happen before a specific time of tribulation. You cannot deny the rapture teaching without denying the Bible. There has to be a time when the dead in Christ are raised, and we who are alive and remain are caught up together with them in the clouds. If that's not true, then you better tear 1 Thessalonians 4 out of your Bible and throw it away."

The rapture is part of biblical teaching. So when someone says, "I don't believe the rapture will happen before the tribulation," that's fine. That's an opinion. That's an interpretation. But when you start making light of the doctrine of the rapture, you're making light of the truthfulness of God's Word and the power of Jesus Christ—and you dare not do that.

Let's look now at seven assurances of the rapture that are present in 1 Thessalonians 4:13-18.

### 1. We Are Not to Grieve as an Unbeliever

In verse 13, Paul writes, "I do not want you to be ignorant, brethren, concerning those who have fallen asleep." He does not want to leave any room for doubt about what is true regarding death. When Paul speaks of "those who have fallen asleep," he doesn't mean people who are literally sleeping. He is using a technical, euphemistic term for death. In Acts 7, when Stephen was stoned to death, the Bible says, "He fell asleep" (verse 60). In that moment, what did Stephen say? "Lord Jesus, receive my spirit" (verse 59). Upon death, a person's body is asleep and in the grave. But the person's spirit is alive. In the case of a Christian, the spirit goes to heaven to be with the Lord.

The very reason Paul desires to address death with the Thessalonians is to remind them that true believers have no reason to grieve like unbelievers. In the minds of unbelievers, there is no hope beyond the grave. Death is the cessation of existence. Once you're dead, the protoplasm is gone. You're done for. There will never be life again.

When I was a young pastor in my twenties, I was asked to oversee a funeral for a teen boy who was killed in an accident. He was not a believer, and I'll never forget his service. In the middle of the funeral, the boy's girlfriend stood up from her seat, ran to the front of the funeral home, and dove into the casket—sobbing and gripping the body. She so disheveled the corpse that others had to pull her off and tidy it up again. That is a picture of an unbeliever filled with sorrow, and God is saying to us, "You don't have to grieve that way."

Now, that doesn't mean we as Christians don't grieve at all when we lose a loved one. Of course our hearts are broken. We miss the person dearly. But we are comforted by the truth that if a person is in Christ, we'll see him or her again. Paul communicates with confident assurance to the church: Possess hope, and do not grieve like an unbeliever.

### 2. We Will Be Reunited with Those Who Have Departed

We have the assurance that the dead in Christ will rise again. Paul writes, "If we believe that Jesus died and rose again, even so God will bring with Him those who sleep in Jesus" (1 Thessalonians 4:14). Here, Paul clearly reiterates the witness of the gospel: Jesus died, then literally rose from the grave. Our Lord didn't just ooze out of the tomb spiritually. Jesus literally walked out of the tomb in a resurrected, glorified body. Yes, the risen Christ could miraculously appear in a room instantly, but He could also say to the disciples: "Touch me and see that I'm real," and "Give Me something to eat" (see Luke 24:36-43). I like those verses!

Jesus said to Thomas, "Reach your finger here, and look at My hands; and reach your hand here, and put it into My side. Do not be unbelieving, but believing" (John 20:27). Jesus rose from the dead in a real, literal body, and so will we. That's the point Paul makes in 1 Thessalonians.

Every theologian who believes the Bible and holds to a historically orthodox Christian view understands that—I don't care what your eschatology is. God's Word teaches that one day, the resurrection of the body will occur. If Jesus died and rose again, so will those who sleep in Jesus.

The *parousia* always refers to the second coming of Christ. In the first phase of the Lord's return, which is the rapture, He will resurrect the dead and give them glorified bodies that will be reunited with their living spirits that had already gone to heaven at the time of their death.

For 20 centuries, faithful believers have lived and then died with faith in Christ. Their spirit immediately goes to heaven. And their body disintegrates in the grave. Even though they have decomposed to dust, and some of them were burned at the stake or eaten by lions, the promise of the Bible is that one day they will rise from the dead and God will miraculously bring their body back to life literally. We are assured that the dead in Christ will return when the Lord Himself calls us up in the rapture.

### 3. We Will Be Reunited with Christ

After stating we are not to grieve like unbelievers and that the dead in Christ will rise again, Paul gives us our third assurance: The Lord Himself will descend from heaven and come back for His own. He will fulfill the promise He made to the disciples in the upper room in John 14. On that day, He will return for you and me—along with all other believers who comprise the bride of Christ—to take us home to the Father's house.

Paul writes, "This we say to you by the word of the Lord, that we who are alive and remain until the coming of the Lord will by no means precede those who are asleep" (1 Thessalonians 4:15). The rapture will not bypass those who have died. The living will not go before them. Jesus will return for every believer. He will resurrect the dead before He raptures those who are alive. But both of these steps will take place so rapidly they will happen almost simultaneously. The dead will rise, and the living will "be caught up together with them in the clouds to meet the Lord in the air" (1 Thessalonians 4:16-17).

### 4. We Will Recognize the Signs

The fourth assurance Paul gives is that there will be signs. We do not know precisely when they will happen, but we know there are three signals involved: the triumphal shout, the voice of an archangel, and the trumpet of God (verse 16). And the result will be a literal resurrection. The text says, "The dead in Christ will rise first" (verse 16). The phrase "in Christ" is used more than 50 times in the New Testament to refer to the bride of Christ, the church. Truly born-again believers are in Christ, and Christ is in them.

The phrase "in Christ" appears only in the New Testament. The term is limited to the bride of Christ, and the promise of the rapture is uniquely for them. The rapture will involve a resurrection of the dead and a snatching up of the living. When the Bridegroom calls from heaven for His bride, He will do so with a shout, with the voice of an archangel, and with the trumpet of God.

### 5. The Rapture Is in Scripture

You'll sometimes hear cynics say, "Raptures are not even in the Bible. Look up the word in a concordance. It's not there." And my response is that neither do we find the word *Trinity* in the Bible. Though it's not there, we still believe in the triune God. Why? Because we see in Scripture that the Father, the Son, and the Holy Spirit all possess the attributes of deity. The concept of the Trinity is present, even if the word is not.

The word *Sunday* also does not appear in the Bible, but Christians worship on Sunday as the Lord's day, or resurrection day. Every Sunday is a celebration of the resurrection of Christ. Again, we understand that the concept is present in Scripture even though the word is not.

While we don't find the word *rapture* in the English Bible, it is found in the Greek New Testament as the word *harpazo*. It literally means "snatched away." You'll find the term in Greek lexicons. So when someone says the word *rapture* is not in the Bible, you can tell them it's in the Greek New Testament. In fact, there are several raptures found in the Bible. The event is not unique to 1 Thessalonians 4.

Enoch walked with God and disappeared (Genesis 5:24; Hebrews 11:5). That's a rapture. Elijah was caught up alive in a chariot of fire (2 Kings 2:11). That's a rapture. In the New Testament, Philip was raptured temporarily after he led the Ethiopian eunuch to Christ on the road to Gaza. Acts 8:39 uses the Greek word *harpazo* to describe how Philip was snatched away and dropped down in another location. Paul himself said, "I was caught up [*harpazo*] to the third heaven"—a temporary rapture—and he saw things he was not allowed to speak about (2 Corinthians 12:2-4).

Notably, the resurrection of Christ and His ascension to heaven are referred to as a rapture in the book of Revelation. In Revelation 12, the apostle John wrote about the male child who was born "to rule all nations." He was "caught up to God and His throne" (verse 5). This verse uses the word *harpazo* to refer to the ascension of Christ.

Also in Revelation, you see the unusual rapture of God's two witnesses in chapter 11. These Jewish prophets will proclaim the gospel to the people of Israel (as will the 144,000 Jewish believers who come from the 12 tribes of Israel). The two witnesses will preach for three-and-a-half years, and at the middle of the tribulation, they will be executed by the antichrist. Their dead bodies will be left on the street in Jerusalem as all the world watches and as people send presents to each other to celebrate their end.

Prior to the twentieth century, it was impossible to imagine how the whole world would be able to witness this event simultaneously. Today's satellite technology makes it possible for everyone to see the same event in real time. You can "be" in Minneapolis, New York, Moscow, Tel Aviv, or Jerusalem—instantly.

Revelation 11:11-12 then describes the rapture of the two witnesses:

> After the three-and-a-half days the breath of life from God
> entered them, and they stood on their feet, and great fear
> fell on those who saw them. And they heard a loud voice
> from heaven saying to them, "Come up here." And they
> ascended to heaven in a cloud, and their enemies saw them."

I'd like to be watching CNN on that day.

Now, why would God go through all the trouble of letting the
witnesses preach, get killed, then resurrect and rapture them? I believe
He will do this to convince people that the greater rapture, the rapture
of the church, had already taken place. During the tribulation, there
will be many unbelievers who claim the reason Christians suddenly
disappeared from earth was because they were abducted by aliens, or
zapped out of existence, or they stepped into another dimension. No;
God came and called the church home before He declared war on the
world. We can rest assured that the rapture described in 1 Thessalonians 4 will happen. Raptures are not a concept foreign to Scripture.

### 6. The Rapture Is a Part of the Second Coming

Some critics of the rapture say, "If you teach that there is a rapture, you're teaching there are two second comings." My response to
them is, "No, we're not." There are two aspects of the second coming, comprising of two separate events. In the rapture of the church,
we will meet the Lord in the air. In the return, Jesus will come to
the earth at the battle of Armageddon to usher in His kingdom. In
Scripture, there are more than 15 differences between the rapture in
the air and the Lord's return to the earth. It's not possible to reconcile them as the same event.

Some people say, "If you are trying to harmonize the differences,
you should look for a harmonistic solution." But if you simply read

the text of the Bible and let it speak for itself, it becomes obvious that there are too many differences for the two events to be one and the same.

For example, when Christ returns, He will come all the way down to the earth. His feet will descend onto the Mount of Olives (Zechariah 14:4). Nobody will be raptured or taken up. At that point, the resurrected saints will not be taken to the Father's house. That will have already occurred. Also, at the return, Christ will come to win the battle of Armageddon. He will come to defeat the beast and the false prophet, and He will judge the world. At the rapture, there is no judgment. This means there are significant differences that are virtually impossible to reconcile.

Now, if the rapture and the return are two separate events, you've got to place the rapture somewhere on the timeline of end-times events. Either the rapture occurs before the tribulation period, in the middle, or at the end. There are some who believe that there is no tribulation period—that the whole church age is the tribulation before the millennium. There are others who say there will be no literal millennium at all. Even so, you still have to place the rapture somewhere. The Bible teaches a rapture of the church, and the only debate is over when it will occur.

By the way, we need to keep in mind that just because other Christians differ with us on the timing of the rapture doesn't mean they are heretics. Though we might disagree, as believers in the family of God, we should show respect for one another's viewpoints about the end times. The only mistake is saying that there is no rapture. The whole point of 1 Thessalonians 4:13-18 is that there will be a reunion in heaven for the family of God at the time of the rapture. The believers who are alive at that moment will be caught up and reunited with those who have already been in heaven, whose bodies were resurrected and reunified with their spirit just moments before.

### 7. We Should Be Encouraged by the Rapture

Our seventh assurance is packaged in this exhortation from Paul: "Therefore comfort one another with these words" (verse 18). The Greek word for "comfort" here comes from the word *paraclete*, "the comforter." The Spirit of God comforts us with the assurance that death is not the end, nor is this world. There is an eternal existence yet to come.

## FOUR PURPOSES OF THE RAPTURE

You may ask, "So what is the purpose of the rapture?" There are at least four reasons it is essential.

One, Christ promised that He would take His bride home to the Father's house (John 14:2-3). Recall what Jesus said: "If I go to the Father's house to prepare a place for you, I will come again for you." Humankind does not know the way, but Jesus said, "I am the way, the truth, and the life" (verse 6).

Two, Romans 14:10-12 says that every believer will stand before the judgment seat of Christ. There must be a time when Christians are taken to heaven to receive their rewards at the judgment seat of Christ. That will occur after the rapture, while the tribulation is taking place here on the earth.

Three, there also needs to be a time when the marriage supper of the Lamb takes place. If you read Revelation 19, you will notice that when believers return with Christ to the earth, they will be wearing "fine linen, white and clean" (verse 14). This tells us that by the time of the second coming, the marriage supper will have already taken place in heaven. The only way it is possible for this to happen is for the church to be raptured to heaven *before* the tribulation.

Four, before the second coming, the bride, or the church, will already have received a white robe of righteousness, which is the gift of God in salvation (verse 8).

This robe of righteousness is not earned by good works. It is a gift given by God's grace to every believer. Where will these robes be obtained? According to verses 7-8, *at* the marriage of the bride to the Bridegroom. The marriage must happen before the return so that the bride can march out of heaven with her warrior husband— no longer the church rejected, persecuted, or martyred. At that time, she will be the church triumphant! The church will come to reign and rule with Christ in His kingdom on earth. For believers to wear white robes at the second coming, there must first be a rapture that takes them up to heaven so they can receive the robes.

## TEN REASONS TO BELIEVE IN A PRE-TRIBULATIONAL RAPTURE

A Pew Research report in 2011 showed that a majority of evangelical Protestant leaders around the globe still believed in the rapture of the church—61 percent.[2] They understand and proclaim this, even though we don't know all the details about the rapture. For example, we do not know what the inhabitants of earth will be up to at the moment the rapture happens. That falls into the category of speculation. Some people believe that the abundance of speculation about the rapture, especially a pre-tribulational one, is reason to reject the idea of a rapture altogether. But no one should reject what is clearly taught in the Bible.

With that said, let me share ten reasons I believe in a pre-tribulational rapture.

First, I appeal to John 14:1-3, where Jesus tells all believers that He will take them to the Father's house. And I look to 1 Thessalonians 4:13-18, where Paul says the dead in Christ will rise first, then those who are alive will go to heaven to be with the Lord. Paul says they will be "caught up" (verse 17). That's the rapture.

Second, Jesus clearly says in Matthew 24:42, "Watch therefore, for you do not know what hour your Lord is coming." Jesus didn't say, "Watch for the tribulation to begin." He didn't say, "Watch for the antichrist." He said, "Watch for Me to come." The only way this makes sense is if the rapture occurs before the tribulation. Only at that time will we have no warning, and therefore, need to be watching.

Third, in Luke 21:36, Jesus tells His followers, "Pray always that you may be counted worthy to escape all these things that will come to pass." He is speaking here about the tribulation. Why would Jesus implore believers to pray for escape if there is no possibility of it? Remember, Jesus promises the church in Philadelphia, "I also will keep you from the hour of trial which shall come upon the whole world" (Revelation 3:10). The little Greek word *ek* ("from") communicates an exit away from. Why would Jesus tell us to pray we will escape the hour of trial if it wasn't possible?

Fourth—and very significantly—in Revelation 12, we read about a woman who is the mother of the Messiah. This persecuted woman symbolizes Israel, not the church. Some Bible teachers get this wrong and surmise that the woman is the church, and say this passage portrays the church, which will flee into the wilderness under persecution. Because symbolic language is used here, we must take care to understand what the symbols mean. The writer of Revelation, John, assumes we've read the Old Testament. The sun, moon, and 12 stars we see on the woman's head (verse 1) are symbols that come right out of the book of Genesis, where we read about Joseph's dream in which his family—that is, Israel, bows down to him (Genesis 37:9). You might ask: "How do you know the woman is Israel and not the church?" Because the woman is described as giving birth to the Messiah, who is the child caught up to the Father's throne (Revelation 12:5). We recognized this earlier when we discussed various examples of raptures that appear in the Bible. Theologians agree the male child in Revelation 12:5 is Jesus.

A problem arises if you view the woman as representing the church.

To say that is to say the church is the mother of Christ. But the church is *not* the mother of Christ; rather, it is the *bride* of Christ. The bride and the mother are two totally different people. How does Matthew 1 begin? With the generations of Jesus Christ, the son of David, the son of Abraham. The Messiah came through the line of Mother Israel. In His flesh, Jesus was Jewish. The church did not establish Christ. Rather, Christ established the church; it was founded by Him.

The fifth reason is the church is not the object of divine wrath. First Thessalonians 5:9 says, "God did not appoint us to wrath, but to obtain salvation through our Lord Jesus Christ." While it is true that the church has always suffered rejection, persecution, and martyrdom, these originate from the wrath of Satan and man. They are not the wrath of God.

When Jesus died on the cross, He shouted, "My God, My God, why have You forsaken Me?" (Matthew 27:46). The wrath of God fell on Him in that moment—God poured out His judgment against our sins. In that moment, He who knew no sin was made sin for us (2 Corinthians 5:21). Jesus took the punishment and wrath of God for us. He loves the bride, and He died for her. The bride is not the object of God's wrath.

Sixth, in the Bible, the rapture is always described as an imminent event. It could happen at any moment. It is the "blessed hope" of the believer (Titus 2:13). It's the good news that we look forward to. It is also described as instantaneous. First Corinthians 15:52 says it will happen "in a moment, in the twinkling of an eye." In a flash—*zap!*—you'll be gone.

Seventh, the rapture is uniquely for those who are in Christ during the church age. If you time the rapture to occur at the end of the tribulation period, then there won't be any saved people left to enter the millennium in their natural bodies. That is a major problem for the post-tribulational rapture viewpoint. If every single believer has been raptured, then everyone will be in a glorified body. So the questions need to be posed: Who will believers rule over in the millennium? And who will give birth to children during the millennium? If the rapture happens at the end of the tribulation, in both cases, the answer is no one.

The eighth reason is that the rapture precedes the bema seat judgment, or Christ's judgment of believers. We see this event in 2 Corinthians 5:10. The rapture must precede the marriage that is to take place before Revelation 19, and it must also precede the battle of Armageddon. The church must be in heaven so believers can receive their rewards, participate in their marriage to the Lamb, and return with Christ to earth when He speaks the word that will "strike the nations" (verse 15). The armies of the antichrist will be slain, and he, along with the false prophet, will be thrown alive into the lake of fire (verse 20). After that, Jesus will reign on earth for 1,000 years (Revelation 20).

How do we know if Scripture really means 1,000 literal years? That's what we are told six times in Revelation 20: "a thousand years" or "the thousand years," repeatedly. With that kind of repetition, we can be sure John means 1,000 years. You may say, "Well, God owns 'the cattle on a thousand hills,' and Psalm 50:10 is obviously describing more than one thousand hills." Yes, in that psalm, the term is used as a figure of speech. But in Revelation 20, we can be sure John is speaking of a literal 1,000 years because at the end of that time, Satan will be let loose to deceive people who have been born during the millennium.

Ninth, I believe the pre-tribulational rapture view does the best job of taking all the pieces of the eschatological puzzle—there are a lot of them—and putting them together in a logical order. The pre-tribulational rapture view does not come out of thin air. No, it comes from carefully studying the Word of God. There must be a time when the dead are raised and the living are caught up so that Christians can go to the judgment seat, marry the Bridegroom, return from heaven with Jesus, and serve with Him during His reign for 1,000 years. Then after Satan's rebellion takes place, we will spend eternity in the new heavens and the new earth, with the New Jerusalem at its center. Also, the pre-tribulational view is the most pro-Israel view because it recognizes the distinction between Israel and the church. It is impossible for replacement theology to rise out of the pre-tribulational view. It can only arise from the other rapture views.

Finally, the bride of Christ is not the object of the Savior's wrath. As we noted in reason five, the church will experience the wrath of men and of Satan, but not the wrath of Jesus. He loves the church, died for the church, and gave Himself for the church. It doesn't make any sense for Christ to beat up His own bride, then marry her.

Christ's love for the church is too great for that to happen. He loves her. He died for her. He gave Himself for her. And hallelujah, He is coming again to take her home to the Father's house.

CHAPTER 7

# ONE MINUTE
# AFTER YOU DIE

ERWIN W. LUTZER

The statistics for death are impressive. No one can avoid it. And there have been many who have wanted to look behind the curtain to know what happens on the other side. There are various ways they attempt to do this.

One is through channeling. There was a man named Bishop James A. Pike whose son committed suicide. Afterward, Pike noticed that when he entered his son's house, the curtains were always pulled in a way that his son liked them, and the clock always stopped at the time that his son had died.

Eventually the father contacted a channeler—a witch—in an attempt to connect with his son. He shared his experiences in a book entitled *The Other Side*.[1] He claims that as he spoke with his son, he asked, "Do you talk about Jesus on the other side?" And the son replied, "No, Dad, we don't talk much about Jesus here." Could I humbly suggest that if a person dies and goes to a place where there isn't much talk about Jesus, they're in deep trouble?

Scripture admonishes us to "give no regard to mediums and familiar spirits" (Leviticus 19:31). These spirits deceive all the unwary who are foolish enough to believe that they can talk with the dead.

Another way people speculate about the other side is through their belief in reincarnation. During an airplane flight some years back, a woman sitting next to me introduced herself. As we talked, she said, "I can prove reincarnation." She then added, "I've never been to the state of Vermont. But I know exactly what the house I grew up in was like during the 1800s." Later in the conversation, I said, "There's no such thing as a transmigration of souls, but there is a transmigration of demons. You are into evil spirits who have deceived you."

She responded, "Oh, I have nothing to do with evil spirits. I welcome only the good ones."

"How do you know they're good?," I asked.

"I receive only those spirits that are clothed in light," she said.

Yet 2 Corinthians 11:14 tells us that "Satan himself transforms himself into an angel of light."

Then there are near-death experiences. As I bring this up, I'm not denying that there are some who may have seen Jesus before they died. Years ago, before certain medications became available, this appears to have happened more often. D.L. Moody reportedly was able to see some of his relatives before he died. According to Acts 7:55-56, as Stephen was being killed, he saw heaven open, with Jesus standing at the right hand of the Father.

Yet there is much deception being spread by those who talk about near-death experiences. For example, author Betty Eadie, who wrote *Embraced by the Light*, claimed that Jesus said it doesn't matter what you believe because there's no judgment day coming. Others have said, "There is a path for Buddhists, a path for Muslims, a path for Christians, and all of them go to the same place." That is outright deception.

## WHAT SCRIPTURE SAYS
## ABOUT LIFE AFTER DEATH

If we want to know what really happens after we die, we must go to Scripture. God's Word is the standard by which we must test everything we read and hear about death. Let's look now at what happens to unbelievers and believers after they die.

### What Happens to Unbelievers After Death?

In the Old Testament, the Hebrew word *Sheol* appears 65 times. In the King James Version of the Bible, this word has been translated 31 times as "the grave," and another 31 times, as "hell." In the remaining three cases, it is translated "the pit." These disparities have caused many people to be confused about the meaning of *Sheol*.

It is clear from the Old Testament that Sheol is a place where the dead go, and it is more than just the grave. It's a place of activity. We know this because there is another Hebrew word that means "grave," and Sheol means more than just that. For example, in Isaiah 14:9-10, we read about Sheol as a place "to meet you at your coming." It's a place where people could expect to meet others. The New Testament equivalent of the Hebrew word *Sheol* is the Greek term *Hades*.

All through the Old Testament, you will find various versions of the phrase "gather you to your fathers" (for example, 2 Kings 22:20). That could refer to putting someone's bones in an ossuary and putting them in a place where the bones of other family members are stored. But the phrase can also speak of a person meeting one's ancestors in the life beyond. For instance, Psalm 73:25 says, "Whom have I in heaven but You? And there is none upon earth that I desire besides You."

The ancient Jews believed there were two compartments in Sheol: one for the righteous and the other for the wicked. A person's destination was determined by whether they had placed their faith in God. I agree with this perspective because it is confirmed in Luke 16, where we read Jesus' account about the rich man and Lazarus. Jesus wanted to show how people's situations can change significantly in the life beyond.

Jesus begins by introducing us to "a certain rich man who was clothed in purple and fine linen and fared sumptuously every day" (Luke 16:19). He had a lot of money and enjoyed life. In contrast was Lazarus, a beggar who sat at the rich man's gate, hoping for "the crumbs which fell from the rich man's table. Moreover the dogs came and licked his sores" (verse 21). After both men died, they went to different destinations. Lazarus was carried by angels to Abraham's bosom, and the rich man went to Hades, where he experienced torment.

Based on what happened to the rich man while he was in Hades, we can know three facts about what unbelievers will experience after they die:

### 1. They Will Be Fully Conscious

"Being in torments in Hades, [the rich man] lifted up his eyes and saw Abraham afar off, and Lazarus in his bosom. Then he cried and said, 'Father Abraham, have mercy on me, and send Lazarus that he may dip the tip of his finger in water and cool my tongue; for I am tormented in this flame'" (verses 23-24). This tells us that people in Hades are conscious. The rich man was fully aware of his surroundings, and he was in pain. By the way, Hades is not hell. We know this because Revelation 20:14 tells us that not until the great white throne judgment in the future will Hades be cast into the lake of fire.

Hades is the destination of unbelievers today. When they get there, they will be fully conscious, and they will face great pain. That's a serious warning to those who do not have salvation in Christ.

I was once asked by an unbelieving family to do a funeral for a wealthy man who died as an atheist. I went to the funeral home, and the son of the deceased told me, "We don't want you to say anything religious. Just make this quick. The only reason you're here is because a relative thought that a pastor should be present."

I made a deal with the son. I said, "I will be brief, but I will talk about Christ because I have to exalt Him. I will not talk about your father."

I preached the gospel for nearly ten minutes. As I did so, I thought to myself, *Even with all the wonderful things these family members might say about this man, what if he could speak to them about where he is right now? I have no doubt that he would plead, "Don't follow me to this place of torment!"*

### 2. Their Destiny Will Be Fixed

Going back to Luke 16, Jesus made it clear that the rich man's destiny was irrevocably fixed. There was nothing he could do to escape. Abraham said to him,

> Remember that in your lifetime you received your good things, and likewise Lazarus evil things; but now he is comforted and you are tormented. And besides all this, between us and you there is a great gulf fixed, so that those who want to pass from here to you cannot, nor can those from there pass to us (verses 25-26).

A great chasm separated the rich man from Lazarus. He couldn't repack his bags and move anywhere else. That will be true about everyone who goes to Hades.

### 3. Their Punishment Will Be Just

The rich man also realized his punishment was just. You might say, "Where does that appear in the text?" Here's why I believe he knew he belonged in Hades: First, he didn't complain that his destination was unjust. And second, he knew exactly what his brothers had to do to *not* end up where he was. The rich man said to Abraham, "I beg you therefore, father, that you would send [Lazarus] to my father's house, for I have five brothers, that he may testify to them, lest they also come to this place of torment" (verses 27-28).

I have heard people say, somewhat flippantly, "I prefer to go to hell because all my friends will be there." But if their friends end up in Hades—later to be thrown into hell—and if those friends were able to speak across the chasm, they would say, "Repent! You don't want to come to this place of torment." That's exactly what the rich man in Luke 16 wanted to tell his brothers.

When it was too late, the rich man in Luke 16 suddenly became interested in missions. He asked, "Please send someone to preach the gospel to my brothers." Some time ago I gave a sermon at a missions conference and I taught from this text, referring to it as a missionary call from Hades to go preach the gospel.

If you were raised Catholic, I want to make an important clarification here. The rich man was not in purgatory. Purgatory is a concept based on a misunderstanding of the doctrine of justification. The idea behind purgatory is that no one dies righteous enough to go into heaven, but they're not bad enough to go into hell either.

Catholicism teaches that purgatory is a place where people are purged of their sins and eventually qualify to enter heaven. I've had Catholics tell me, "As long as I make it to purgatory, no matter how long it is, eventually, I'll get into heaven."

But that's not what the Bible says. Scripture teaches that justification by faith involves receiving Christ as Savior and having His righteousness credited to us. Because we have His righteousness, we are instantly welcomed into heaven just as if we were Jesus.

### What Happens to Believers After Death?

Did you know that for believers, death is a great blessing? In 1 Corinthians 3:21-22, Paul wrote, "All things are yours: whether... the world or life or death." He lists death as a gift of God. Death is the means by which God brings His children into His presence.

### We Will Still Be the Same Person and Remember One Another

After you die, you'll be the same person you are here. You'll have the same personality. You'll be different because you'll be without sin, but you'll still be the person God created you to be.

Widows and widowers often ask me, "Will my spouse remember me on the other side?" I tell them, "Do you think your spouse will know less in heaven than they did on earth? Yes, they will remember you. And they will remember all family relationships."

We know this is true because the rich man in Luke 16 remembered his five brothers after he went to Hades. However, while spouses will remember each other, their relationship with one another will be different because in heaven, there will be no marriage. As Jesus said in Matthew 22:30, "In the resurrection they neither marry nor are given in marriage."

### We Will Go from the Temporary to the Eternal

The apostle Paul described our body as a collapsing tent. He wrote that when our "earthly house, this tent, is destroyed, we have a building from God, a house not made with hands, eternal in the heavens" (2 Corinthians 5:1). Tents are a temporary dwelling place. Over time, they wear out. They leak, and the canvas becomes tattered.

But someday, we will live in a permanent home. Jesus said, "In My Father's house are many mansions...I go to prepare a place for you" (John 14:2). And we'll be given crowns to wear. Heaven will be a special place!

There was a little girl who was reading stories about Jesus with her mother. That night, she had a dream. The next morning, the girl told her mother, "Oh, Mommy! I dreamed about Jesus, and He is so much better than the pictures." Likewise, heaven will be so much better than the pictures.

### We Will Enter Jesus' Presence Immediately

Many people have misconceptions about what happens to the body and soul after death. There are some who believe in what is called soul sleep. They say that between death and heaven, we will be suspended in an intermediate state.

But that's not supported by Scripture. In Philippians 1:23, Paul said he had "a desire to depart and be with Christ, which is far better." To depart is to die, at which time Paul would be in Christ's presence. He wouldn't have said this if he expected to lie in the grave until the day of resurrection.

Remember what happened to Stephen? As he was being stoned to death, he saw heaven open, with Jesus "standing at the right hand of God," ready to receive him (Acts 7:55). When he saw the heavens open, Jesus was standing ready to welcome him. Stephen did not go into soul sleep.

Consider the thief who was crucified alongside Jesus. Convicted of his sin, in repentance, he cried out to Jesus, "Lord, remember me when You come into Your kingdom." Jesus answered, "Today you will be with Me in Paradise" (Luke 23:42-43). That very night, he was supping with Jesus in Paradise. What grace!

Scripture affirms that after death, our soul enters Jesus' presence immediately. But what about our physical body? There are some who say we will be given intermediate bodies because of how Moses and Elijah showed up with Jesus on the Mount of Transfiguration. Also, the rich man in Luke 16 had eyes and ears and was able to feel pain.

But then that intermediate body would have to be discarded on the day of resurrection, or at the rapture. I personally believe that, after death, a person's soul takes on the characteristics of his or her body, and that those who are in heaven now have a sense of incompleteness. They are awaiting the day of resurrection that is still to come so that their souls can be rejoined to their glorified bodies.

Notice what happens to those who will be killed during the tribulation. Revelation 6:9-10 makes it clear that it is their souls that are present before God in heaven. It is "the *souls* of those who had been slain for the word of God" that will cry out to Him, saying, "How long, O Lord, holy and true, until You judge and avenge our blood on those who dwell on the earth?"

Apparently these believers who had been slain for their faith do not yet have their resurrection bodies. But they are able to cry out to God, which seems to indicate their souls take on characteristics of their bodies so that they can see the Lord and communicate to Him. That is my personal view.

As for the body, 1 Corinthians 15:42-44 says, "The body is sown in corruption, it is raised in incorruption. It is sown in dishonor, it is raised in glory. It is sown in weakness, it is raised in power. It is sown a natural body, it is raised a spiritual body." That's not saying we're going to be spirits in heaven, but that someday we'll have a body like the one we have now, but in a glorified state. Our bodies will be amazingly better. We'll never get tired. If you want to go somewhere, a mere thought will immediately transport you there. In the same way the risen Jesus was able to go instantly from one place to another, you will too. That's a small taste of what heaven will be like.

What about children who die young, including infants? I believe that when they die, they go to heaven. Jesus said, "Let the little children come to Me, and do not forbid them; for of such is the kingdom of heaven" (Matthew 19:14). And in Matthew 18:10, He said, "Do not despise one of these little ones, for I say to you that in heaven their angels always see the face of My Father who is in heaven." That puts children close to the throne of God.

When it comes to children and their eternal destiny, some people wonder about the age of accountability. The Bible does not comment on what this age might be. It likely varies with different people, and we can be certain God knows their hearts perfectly. There are also people with physical and mental disabilities who I believe will be in heaven because they never attain the age of understanding and personal responsibility. This is a matter we need to entrust to God.

### We Will Be One Big Family

Finally, in heaven, we are going to be one big family—the family of God. Jesus said, "Who is My mother and who are My brothers?…Here are My mother and My brothers! For whoever does the will of My Father in heaven is My brother and sister and mother" (Matthew 12:48-50). Jesus was not talking about nuclear families like we have here on earth. He was saying that we will all be part of the family of God.

## WHAT SCRIPTURE SAYS
## ABOUT FINAL JUDGMENT

The ominous side to all this talk about life after death is the fact that the unsaved will not eventually cease to exist. They will be raised up to face final judgment, and they will be punished forever. Daniel 12:2 says, "Those who sleep in the dust of the earth shall awake, some to everlasting life, some to shame and everlasting contempt."

This brings us to one of the most foreboding passages in all the Bible, in Revelation chapter 20:

> I saw a great white throne and Him who sat on it, from whose face the earth and the heaven fled away. And there was found no place for them. And I saw the dead, small and great, standing before God, and books were opened. And another book was opened, which is the Book of Life. And the dead were judged according to their works, by the things which were written in the books. The sea gave up the dead who were in it, and Death and Hades delivered up the dead who were in them. And they were judged, each one according to his works. Then Death and Hades were cast into the lake of fire. This is the second death. And anyone not

found written in the Book of Life was cast into the lake of fire (verses 11-15).

Before I explain this passage, I want to comment briefly about a popular book titled *Love Wins: A Book About Heaven, Hell, and the Fate of Every Person Who Ever Lived.*[2] The author denies the eternality of hell and conscious punishment. While we may wish that everyone could end up in heaven, we must remember that we are not the ones who decide our eternal destiny. God is God, and we're not. We have to bow before everything Scripture says, and that includes its serious statements about death and judgment.

Try to visualize the scene described here in Revelation 20. A crowd too great to count stands before God. Both rich and poor will be here. Kings will stand beside servants. There will be people from many different religious backgrounds. Some will never have been arrested, while others will be murderers.

What will they all have in common? They will lack the kind of righteousness that God requires for them to enter heaven. Imagine you are in that crowd. You will know, in advance, what the verdict will be. You're headed for the lake of fire. At this point, there is no possibility of changing your destination. It will be too late.

Before you are two books. One is the book of life, and the other is a book in which everyone's deeds are recorded. We know that no one can be saved by good deeds. Those who enter heaven will do so "not by works of righteousness which [they] have done, but according to His mercy" (Titus 3:5). Though we cannot be saved by our deeds, we will be judged by them.

For those who wonder whether God will judge fairly, Scripture reveals hell will not be the same for everyone. In Luke 12:47-48, Jesus said, "That servant who knew his master's will and did not prepare himself or do according to his will, shall be beaten with many stripes. But he who did not know, yet committed things deserving of stripes, shall be beaten with few." People will be judged on the basis of what they did with what they knew. Those who generally tried to live a good life will face less punishment than those who were truly intentional about evil and perpetuating it.

In Matthew 9:42, Jesus said, "Whoever causes one of these little ones who believe in Me to stumble, it would be better for him if a millstone were hung around his neck, and he were thrown into the sea." Some will receive greater judgment because of how they treated others. And I don't believe there will be anyone in hell who will say their punishment is unfair. They will know that God's judgment is perfectly just.

At the judgment described in Revelation 20, no one will be saved. Verse 13 says they will be judged "each one according to his works"— every one of them. Then we're told of their fate: "Death and Hades were cast into the lake of fire" (verse 15).

Some people ask, "Isn't this overkill? Sure, these people sinned, but isn't this too much?"

Think of it this way: Jonathan Edwards is reported to have said that the greatness of a sin is dependent on the greatness of the being against whom it is committed. For example, if you throw a snowball at your sibling, that's no big deal. If you throw one at a parent, that might be a problem. To throw a snowball at a law officer would get you in trouble. And if you throw one at the president of the United States, you would be arrested. Why? Because the higher you go up the ladder, the worse the offense becomes. Using that analogy, think of the infinite crime of sinning against an infinite God.

One reason people fail to grasp the justness of God's judgment is because they have absolutely no idea of the extent to which God hates sin. Deuteronomy 32:4 says of God, "His work is perfect, for all His ways are justice. A God of truth and without injustice; righteous and upright is He."

God is so perfectly just that He cannot be unjust.

## OVERCOMING THE FEAR OF DEATH

D.L. Moody said there was a time in his life when he was terrified of dying. But later, that changed. And when it came time for him to die, he was no longer afraid. In fact, we are told that among his last words were these: "Earth recedes, heaven opens before me. If this is death, it is sweet!" Moody knew it was time for him to die, and that he would immediately be in the presence of Jesus.

If you are a Christian, when you die, you will see Jesus. He will welcome you into His presence. I believe you will also see angels. Remember what Luke 16 said about the beggar? After he died, he was "carried by the angels to Abraham's bosom" (verse 22).

We can expect that we will see others whom we knew on earth, although Scripture doesn't tell us about the nature of the relationships we will have with them. But we will love and know one another.

And what about those who don't show up in heaven? There will be parents whose children aren't there. And husbands or wives whose spouses are not in heaven. How will that affect us? Revelation 21:4 gives the assurance that "God will wipe away every tear" from our eyes. I believe this applies to any kind of sadness we might experience in heaven—sadness over those who aren't there, over deep regrets we might have, over pain and suffering. The Greek text in this passage tells us God will wipe our tears all the way to the very roots of our grief.

## THE DIFFERENCE JESUS MAKES

Some years ago, I had the privilege of speaking at a church in Washington, DC. A member of the Secret Service was there, and asked me, "Would you like to visit the Oval Office?" At the time, the president was out of town, so he wasn't in the White House. The Secret Service agent said, "If you show up on Monday, I can get you into the Oval Office."

That next morning, our little group showed up at the White House. In those days, security wasn't as tight as it is now. We were with the

Secret Service agent, and one of the guards at the security hut looked at us and said, "Oh, you're with him? Go on in."

At the door of the White House, there were more guards. Looking at the agent, they said, "You're with him? Go right on in." We walked to the Oval Office, where a guard stood at attention. When he saw the agent, he motioned for us to enter. We were not allowed to go near the president's desk, but we did step into the office.

As all this happened, a thought occurred to me. Some Christians are afraid of death because of what they've done in their past. They're fearful because of serious sins they committed. Perhaps they had addictions they struggled over. Or they aborted a child or committed sexual immorality. And even though they're aware that those who confess Christ as Savior have been forgiven, still, they say to themselves, "I can't go in."

But an angel will say, "Because you're with Jesus, come on in."

That's why we sing, "Dressed in his righteousness alone, faultless to stand before the throne."[3] As believers, we have been made holy in Christ. We are saved entirely by His power and grace, and He gives us His righteousness.

When Jesus is with us as our Savior, we will be welcomed into heaven.

CHAPTER 8

# A WARNING TO AMERICA FROM THE BOOK OF JOEL

## ANNE GRAHAM LOTZ

On April 10, 1912, the greatest, largest, most luxurious ship ever to be built set sail from Southampton, England—the *Titanic*. At first, this maiden voyage was uneventful, and the ship went through calm seas. But on April 14, that changed. The *Titanic* received seven telegraph messages that day from other ships about icebergs and ice floes, saying, "Go around, change your course. It's dangerous."

In the meantime, the telegraph operator on the *Titanic* was busy. People were partying and having a good time. They were sending and receiving telegrams from all their friends in Europe and the United States, telling them what they were doing. In between all those messages, the telegraph operator received the warnings—all of them. But he didn't heed them. At 11:40 on the night of April 14, the *Titanic* hit an iceberg. And at 2:20, early in the morning of April 15, two hours and 40 minutes later, the ship went down into the sea, and the rest is history.

In the same way, our ship of state is headed toward an iceberg. The warnings have come, one after another: Turn around. Change course.

You're headed toward disaster. But we don't see America changing course. And it's more than just America. Even much of the church isn't heeding the warnings. God is alerting us, and the warning is this: Judgment is coming. We see all that is happening in the Middle East as well as globally. It's eye-opening, isn't it?

While the warnings are relevant for the entire world, I want us to focus on our beloved nation of America because I believe time is running out. Let's look together at Joel chapter 1, and see what God says there. In my Bible, this text has underlining and notes, as well as tear stains. With great urgency, Joel says, "Wake up!"

The warnings are credible, comprehensive, and compelling. That's the outline we will follow, starting with the fact the warnings are credible.

## THE WARNINGS ARE CREDIBLE

Joel 1:1 begins by telling us we are reading "the word of the LORD." The message here is indisputable because it is from the Lord. You can take God at His word. He means what He says, and He says what He means. He does not lie.

The warnings in the book of Joel are credible because they are from God. We then read that this word "came to Joel son of Pethuel" (verse 1). We don't know much about Joel. He was the son of Pethuel. And he was a prophet who warned of a coming invasion and destruction against God's people. Though his message was preached long ago, his words transcend time. What he said is for all people for all time, including us.

Joel 1:2 goes on to say, "Hear this." There is nothing more important that you and I can do than listen to the Word of God, especially when our nation is provoking God's judgment. We need to be listening to, reading, applying, and obeying what God says.

Noah comes to mind here. You will remember that according to Genesis 6, Noah was living in a world saturated with evil. As verse 5 tells us, "The LORD saw that the wickedness of man was great in the earth, and that every intent of the thoughts of his heart was only evil." Noah was the only man on the planet who was righteous and blameless. He walked with God, which means he listened to God and took the time to talk with God about what He said. That's the kind of fellowship they had with each other.

I go for walks at home with a friend. When we go out during the morning, we walk at the same pace, in the same direction, so we can stay together. When you walk with God, you want to make sure you walk at His pace, step by step, in obedience to His Word, which you need to take the time to read. As you listen to what He says and walk at His pace, you also want to walk in His direction. You surrender your will to Him. You don't want to follow your own agendas or goals.

As Noah walked with God, the Lord impressed upon Noah's heart the fact judgment was coming. He said, "I'm grieved that I made man. I'm going to send a flood to destroy the whole world." God also told Noah that He would make salvation available to anyone who wanted to be spared from judgment. Anyone who was willing to enter the ark would be saved.

Noah did exactly what God told him to do. He built an ark that would save himself, his family, and every kind of animal. If Noah hadn't been walking with God and obeying Him, you and I wouldn't be here today. Because Noah listened to God and applied what He said, Noah's family was saved, and the human race was spared. The rest of the world, however, provoked God's judgment.

We live in a nation that is incurring God's wrath. And we cannot do anything more important than reading, applying, and obeying God's Word. It's as we walk with the Lord that He impresses us with what's on His heart and mind. As someone who walks with God, I can tell you judgment is on His mind. But so is salvation.

God told Noah judgment was coming in the land. But then He

told Noah to build an ark that would provide salvation from judgment to anyone who would choose to enter. It's an Old Testament message of the gospel.

Don't let a day go by without reading your Bible. Don't do this just to learn facts and information. Read your Bible so you can hear God speaking to you through it. Someone's salvation from judgment may depend on it.

## THE WARNINGS ARE COMPREHENSIVE

The warnings in God's Word are credible because they're undisputable. They're also comprehensive, or for everyone. Joel 1:2 says, "Give ear, all you inhabitants of the land!" These warnings are for old and young. They're for all generations. They are for those who read on the printed page or follow along on iPods and iPhones.

God's words of coming judgment are for all sinners. We read in Joel 1:9-13 that His words are for priests and religious leaders as well—for those who are strict on everybody else and think they're right before God when they aren't. They do all their good deeds for themselves, not for God.

Verse 11 adds that God's warnings are also for farmers, or the working people. Verse 14 says they are for "all the inhabitants of the land." While these words are directed at God's people, they are also for those everywhere, including America. But in particular, God's people should have the ears to hear and the eyes to see what God is up to.

There are many who will be caught by surprise when judgment falls. Don't you be among them. God has given us enough warnings so that we can know judgment is coming and we can be prepared.

In Joel 1:2, the prophet asks, "Has anything like this happened in your days, or even in the days of your fathers?" That implies nothing like the forthcoming judgments has ever been experienced by Joel's listeners. Joel, of course, was speaking about a plague of locusts, among other terrible disasters. Today's generations have also faced disasters that have never happened before. Consider 9/11, when the Twin Towers collapsed and the Pentagon was hit. Those who witnessed the events of that day will never forget them.

That is one example of a warning shot across the bow—a shot meant to wake up America. And people did wake up for a while. They went to church. They prayed. There was a wonderful unity as people recognized we were all affected by this tragedy.

But then the enemy put his spin on what had happened. We were told we needed to be inclusive and tolerant. We were told to be careful to avoid offending those who believe differently than us even though 9/11 had been perpetuated by Islamist extremists who carried out terrorists acts because of their beliefs.

Then as time went on, 9/11 faded from people's memories.

Later came Hurricane Katrina. I remember going online and watching a fast-forward film of the hurricane as it swept through New Orleans. And it was like watching God setting off alarms, trying to wake up people and warn them.

There have been other major disasters since. That is what the book of Joel is about: Judgment is coming, and God is giving us warnings. These warnings are credible because they are from God. Ultimately, these judgments will affect every area of our world, including America. We see in the Old Testament that when God could no longer get His people's attention through the prophets and His Word, He sent disasters upon them.

In Joel 1:4, we read about judgment God sent in the form of a plague of locusts: "What the chewing locust left, the swarming locust has eaten; what the swarming locust left, the crawling locust has eaten; and what the crawling locust left, the consuming locust has eaten." This describes the different stages of the devastation left by locusts. Every stage was destructive, and eventually, there was nothing left in the land. It was stripped bare.

This was a massive environmental disaster. We've also had record-breaking environmental disasters in our time as well. For example, in 2015, there were serious floods and tornadoes in Oklahoma and Texas. There were numerous wildfires from California to Montana. Major flooding in South Carolina led Governor Nikki Haley to say the state had faced "a storm of historic proportions."[1]

A year later, there was flooding in Louisiana that was worse than that experienced during Hurricane Katrina. On August 24, 2016, 22 tornadoes touched down in Ohio and Indiana.[2] A couple months later, Hurricane Matthew swept through my home state of North Carolina. I was at home as trees came down and the power went out. Everything was a mess. The next day, the sky was blue, but the destruction was widespread. The flooding continued to worsen, and entire towns were devastated.

These are just a few examples of the kinds of environmental disasters that are on the increase. Through them, God is saying, "Wake up!"

Joel 1:5 speaks of societal disasters, which can include substance abuse, such as drug addiction and alcoholism. Here, we read, "Awake, you drunkards, and weep; and wail, all you drinkers of wine."

The statistics are constantly changing, but I will share some of the latest. And we can be sure they will continue to get worse.

Alcohol-related accidents are the leading cause of traffic fatalities in the United States, with more than 10,000 lives lost each year.[3] Did you know that? Some 15 million people struggle with alcoholism in the US, and "more than 88,000 people die from alcohol-related deaths."[4] Alcohol is often involved in many of today's crimes—40 percent of child beatings, 27 percent of aggravated assaults, 37 percent of sexual assaults and rape, and 40 percent of murders.[5]

Drug abuse has brought disaster as well, and it's getting worse because of the increasing legalization of marijuana. Teenage marijuana use is now at its highest level in 30 years.[6] We know that marijuana has been proven to lead to affect a person's thinking abilities and moods, and for teens, it affects brain development.[7] Those who use it are less likely to graduate.[8] And yet about two-thirds of high school seniors say they see no harm in marijuana.[9] That's a disaster! Drug overdose is now a leading cause of accidental death in America. An estimated 106,000 people died of overdoses in 2021.[10] That was more than guns and car accidents combined. Suicide is the third-leading cause of death among 15- to 24-year-olds.[11] Active shooter incidents have increased in number as well.

There have been financial crises too. In recent decades, we've seen the bankruptcy of Lehman Brothers and the collapse of Fannie Mae and Freddie Mac due to a housing crash. People worry that downturns in the financial markets can wipe out a lot of their retirement savings. Over the past several years, we've seen real wages decline due to the effects of inflation.[12] Purchasing power has diminished, and credit card debt has increased to record levels.[13] Many people have no emergency savings. And student loan debt has crippled an entire generation of college graduates.

The US national debt continues to spiral out of control. At the time of this writing, it's rapidly approaching $35 trillion. That's $102,800 for every person living in the United States.[14] And the Congressional Budget Office says that debt will continue to skyrocket another $2 trillion per year for the next decade.[15]

Joel 1:6-7 talks about national disaster. In verse 6, God says, "A nation has come up against My land." I don't want to get political by saying this, but there's a very real invasion taking place now in the US. There are some who call this immigration, or open borders, or taking care of refugees. Europe is being invaded as well by immigrants from predominantly Muslim countries in North Africa and the Middle East.

Then there is the plague of pornography. Some people estimate this industry makes more money per year than Apple, Google, Microsoft, and Amazon combined.[16] It is big business. Pornography is like the creeping black mold that results after a hurricane has flooded homes and caused enormous amounts of water damage. People have to tear out their walls and insulation to stop the mold that has a poisonous effect on them. Pornography eats away at the underpinnings of our nation. If you're indulging in it, I urge you to stop. You may think it is harmless, but it will destroy your spirit. As Jesus said, "If your right eye causes you to sin, pluck it out and cast it from you; for it is more profitable for you that one of your members perish, than for your whole body to be cast into hell" (Matthew 5:29).

We're also faced with hatred and racial division in this country. And it's getting worse. There are people who have racial agendas, and instead of helping to bring everyone together, they are pushing people apart. We're seeing antisemitism soar, especially on college campuses. After the Holocaust, you would think this wouldn't happen. And yet we are seeing dramatic rises in antisemitism. There was a 400 percent rise in antisemitic incidents in the US during the first two weeks after Hamas's October 7, 2023, attack against Israel.[17]

We're also seeing growing numbers of people affected by secularism, humanism, atheism, and agnosticism. People lack faith in God and a fear of God. Even within the church, Christians have lost their reverence for God, turning Him into a big buddy in the sky.

In Joel 1:9, we read, "The grain offering and the drink offering have been cut off from the house of the LORD." Sacrificial offerings ceased because there was nothing left to sacrifice. This refers to spiritual disaster. After people go through other kinds of disasters like 9/11 and hurricanes and economic collapses, they ask, "Where is God? Why didn't He keep this from happening? Doesn't He care?" People wonder whether God has abandoned them, but He hasn't. He is always there.

Even during disasters, God is at work. While there are some who don't survive—including loved ones and friends—there are many others who do. Nearly 3,000 people died on 9/11, but there were

50,000 people who worked in those two towers.[18] While just one death is too many, we have to realize God works in ways we don't understand. When we get to heaven, we will find out more. But God does show up. He does care. He sees, and He loves people, and He promises His presence.

When we go through the valley of the shadow of death, God will be with us (Psalm 23:4). When we go through the waters, we won't be overwhelmed, and when we go through the fire, we won't be burned (Isaiah 43:2). God assures us of His presence, even though we may feel we have been abandoned.

I've had times when I have felt abandoned—when it seemed as if God was not near. But then I am reminded of Hebrews 13:5, where God says, "I will never leave you nor forsake you." I find it helpful to put my name in that passage. We can be sure God keeps His promises no matter how we feel. We are to live by faith, not feelings.

The conditions Joel describes fit what we see happening in America. The darkness has become oppressive. And a lot of it is spiritual in nature. In Joel 1:12, the prophet says, "Surely joy has withered away from the sons of men." When people go through disasters and lose their material things or pleasures, they lose their joy because it's wrapped up in those things. But when your joy is in Jesus, you will never lose it.

Joel lamented, "The field is wasted, the land mourns; for the grain is ruined...Be ashamed, you farmers, wail, you vinedressers, for the wheat and the barley, because the harvest of the field has perished. The vine has dried up, and the fig tree has withered" (1:10-12). We've all seen pictures of sunbaked fields, or land that is flooded. Just like that, God can send a plague or a flood or a drought. An agricultural disaster could hit, and people would find the grocery store shelves empty.

These are the kinds of warnings God sends. Judgment is coming, and people need to wake up. While disasters have always happened, they are becoming more severe. Yes, it is true that God is merciful.

He is kind. He is patient. And He is forgiving, not willing that any should perish (2 Peter 3:9).

But God is also holy, righteous, and just. Eventually there will come a point when He says, "Enough!" As He said in Genesis 6:3, "My Spirit shall not strive with man forever." Once God removes His Spirit, there's no restraint for evil. I'm not talking about when the Spirit is removed at the time all believers are raptured. I believe we are now seeing the kind of judgment described in Romans 1:18-32. When people refuse to repent and they continue in their sin, God removes His hand of protection and blessing from them because they are of a reprobate mind. That's when chaos and confusion and catastrophe strike.

That's what we see happening in America. Many people don't want God. They think they don't need Him. They have taken Him out of the schools, the government, and the marketplace. They are shaking their fists at Him, saying, "Get out!" And God departs with tears because He knows what's coming.

### THE WARNINGS ARE COMPELLING

God's warnings stir you and me to cry out and let people know there is still hope. Why would God warn people if there wasn't an opportunity to turn things around? He could go ahead and send judgment immediately. Instead, God warns us. He doesn't sneak up and judge us by surprise. He warns us in advance and puts us on notice. Look at Joel 2:12: " 'Now, therefore,' says the LORD." Even at this late hour, He says, "Turn to Me with all your heart, with fasting, with weeping, and with mourning. So rend your heart, and not your garments" (verses 12-13).

Back in Joel 1:13, God said, "Gird yourselves…in sackcloth." To do this was to give outward evidence that inwardly, one was desperate for God. At this point, truly repentant people will say, "God, if

You don't get us out of this mess, we're not going to get out. If You don't save us, we won't be saved. If You don't bless us, we won't be blessed. If You don't come down in our midst and give us a sense of Your presence and Your peace, we'll never have peace. We'll never have unity or reconciliation."

Joel 1:14 then speaks of fasting or going without food. When I fast, I go without anything at all and get on my face before God. I focus all my attention on Him. That's what fasting is about—getting alone with God and praying.

All of us should do this. When was the last time you fasted and spent time in prayer? We should take time to get together with others and pray to the Lord. We should put on our spiritual sackcloth and pray that people will seek Him. If our nation is coming under the judgment of God, the only remedy is repentance from sin, not political change.

In Joel 1:15, the prophet warned, "The day of the Lord is at hand." Judgment was imminent. The day of the Lord is a time when God has had enough. That's when He says, "My patience has run out. The day of accountability and reckoning has arrived."

In history, there have been other days of judgment—such as when the Assyrians destroyed the northern kingdom of Israel, or the Babylonians conquered the southern kingdom of Judah. In AD 70, nearly 40 years after Jesus' crucifixion, the Romans wiped out Jerusalem and destroyed the temple. And in the future, there is coming that great and terrible day of the Lord when Jesus returns. I believe that a coming day of judgment is near for America.

It's possible that could happen in connection with the rapture. When all the believers in America are suddenly gone, that's going to be a form of judgment itself. Can you imagine the impact that will have? So many people will be gone all at once that our country will collapse.

Yet I have wondered if, before that happens, God will allow us to experience a judgment that helps to purify the church. Things may happen that put enough pressure on people to look up to God. That's why we should always be ready to share the gospel. God may allow America to go through some crises so that He can get people's attention and cause them to open their ears to the gospel.

Joel then goes on to say, "The day of the LORD...shall come as destruction from the Almighty. Is not the food cut off before our eyes, joy and gladness from the house of our God?" (1:15-16). God's warnings are obvious. They're meant to get people to open their eyes and cry out to Him. As verse 19 says, "O LORD, to You I cry out." This reminds us of when God's children were in bondage and slavery in Egypt. After Joseph died and years had gone by, along came a Pharaoh who did not remember Joseph. This Pharaoh enslaved God's people, and they cried out to Him. God heard their cry, and He sent Moses to deliver them.

After the Israelites were let free, they left Egypt. They headed toward the Red Sea. Pharaoh then changed his mind and sent his army after the Hebrews, who cried out to God once again. God opened the Red Sea so the people could cross on dry ground.

All through the many years in the wilderness, God cared for His people. When the time finally came for them to conquer Jericho, God told them to march around the city for seven days. On the seventh day, they circled Jericho seven times, then blew trumpets—and the walls came tumbling down, leading to the defeat of Israel's enemy.

Then there was Gideon. To the Hebrews, the enemy that gathered appeared as thick as locusts on the land (Judges 7:12). God winnowed down Gideon's army until there were only 300 men remaining. They were told to go into battle with clay jars, trumpets, and torches. When the Israelites blew their trumpets and broke the clay jars, the Midianites became frightened, and were defeated.

God also protected the prophet Elijah during and after his encounter on Mount Carmel with the priests of Baal. Elijah taunted the priests, urging them to get Baal to send down fire from heaven to burn their sacrificial offering. Nothing happened. When it was Elijah's turn to call down fire from heaven, he got down on his face and pleaded, "Hear me, O Lord, hear me, that this people may know that You are the Lord God" (1 Kings 18:37). After he prayed, fire came down immediately and consumed the offering Elijah had prepared.

Even after Jonah rebelled against God and refused to go to Nineveh, God spared Jonah from the belly of a fish. I can't think of a worse place to be! Jonah repented of his disobedience and cried out to God, and the Lord delivered him.

And we all know what happened while Jesus was hanging on the cross. He pleaded, "My God, My God, why have You forsaken Me?" (Matthew 27:46). Then He said, "Father, into Your hands I commit My spirit" (Luke 23:46), and "It is finished!" (John 19:30). Jesus then bowed His head and died. Three days later, the Father raised Him from the dead, all because He hears the cries of His people.

Psalm 34:17 says, "The righteous cry out, and the Lord hears, and delivers them out of all their troubles." That is still true about God today. He is the same as He was in Moses' day, Elijah's day, Daniel's day, Jonah's day, and Joel's day. He was and is and will be the same yesterday, today, and tomorrow. He is the God of creation, redemption, salvation, compassion, and mercy and forgiveness. He is just, kind, righteous, and gracious. And He loves to hear His people cry out! He will hear and answer us, but first, we must cry.

I believe with all my heart that it is time for us as God's people to humble ourselves and to pray, to seek God's face, and to turn from our wicked ways. And He will hear our prayer. He has promised He would. He will forgive our sin and He will heal our land.

We usually think about judgment as sometime in the future. But we have no way of knowing when we will step into eternity. Who knows when we might get into a car accident, or have a heart attack? Several years ago, I found my husband of 49 years unresponsive in our pool. On that day, I had no idea he was going to enter eternity. But he did, and I praise God that he was ready.

Are you ready? What if judgment is about to come for you and call you into eternity? If you've never gone to the cross and claimed Jesus as your Savior and asked Him to cleanse you of your sin and come into your heart, you need to surrender your life to Him. You need to get right with God now. Don't wait until later. You never know how much time you have left.

If that's the desire of your heart now, would you pray a prayer along these lines?

> God, I want to be saved from Your judgment. I'm sorry for my sin and I want to repent and turn away from it. I need Your help. I believe Jesus died on the cross so that His blood would cleanse me and forgive me of all my sin. I believe Jesus rose on the third day to conquer sin and death, and that He has the power to give me eternal life. I receive eternal life in His name. I claim a personal relationship with You that will never end. I open my heart and invite You to come live in me, never to leave me. No matter what happens to this nation or this world, I know that You will live inside of me and You will take care of me. And from this moment onward, I choose to live my life for You.

The Bible says that if you confess your sin, God is faithful and just and He will cleanse you (1 John 1:9). If you ask Him to give you eternal life, He will. And He will never leave nor forsake you (Hebrews 13:5).

Whether you are a new Christian or you have already been one, you can thank God that Jesus sent the Holy Spirit to live within you. You can know that with certainty because God's Word is credible. And if you're coming to the cross for the first time, God has heard your cry, and heaven is rejoicing over you.

Together, let's thank the Lord for the privilege of living in this dangerous day. This is such a strategic time in our nation's history. We have the privilege of sharing the gospel and the reason for the hope that is within us. We've been called to share the Word of the Lord, the gospel, to help people make sense out of the confusion, and show them the light at the end of the tunnel.

> Lord, we pray for the glory of Your name as the church cries out to You. Help us to stand in the gap for America. God, we give You the glory and the praise and the honor because You alone are worthy. In the name of our Lord and Savior Jesus Christ we pray, amen.

CHAPTER 9

# APOSTASY: THE SABOTAGE OF CHRISTIANITY FROM WITHIN

## MARK HITCHCOCK

I n 1813, the second president of the United States, John Adams, wrote these words to his vice president, Thomas Jefferson: "My friend, you and I have lived in serious times."[1]

These two patriots had indeed lived in serious times. They, along with many others, had staked their lives on the success of a revolution against the British Empire. Thomas Paine expressed that same sentiment back in 1776 when he wrote, "These are the times that try men's souls."[2]

I believe that today, we can look around us and say, "We live in serious times. We live in the times that try men's souls." Our world is rapidly becoming more insecure and unstable politically, culturally, morally, economically, and spiritually.

One night while I was watching the news, a commentator said, "There's a sense that everything is closing in on us." I thought, *That's an interesting way to put it.* Even people who don't know the Lord or the Bible have this sense that the world is getting nearer to closing time. Back in 2017, *USA Today* featured an article headlined "Storms, earthquakes, North Korea and now the Las Vegas massacre. We have to wonder: 'What's next?'" The article opened, "When the month began, a confluence of hurricanes, floods, earthquakes, wildfires and a brewing international nuclear confrontation already had some Americans thinking about the End Times." The article concluded with a statement from a pastor in Tulsa, Oklahoma, who said, "With all that's going on in the world, you can't help but be a little bit apocalyptic."[3]

Though our world faces many dangers today, there is one threat that I believe weighs more heavily on God's heart than all the others: apostasy within the church.

More and more, we're seeing a falling away that is taking place within professing Christendom. And Scripture makes it clear that our Lord's chief concern is for His church here on earth. That's because the church is the body and the bride of Christ. Therefore, anything that threatens His church will be a serious concern to Him.

As much as we might be distressed about what's happening in today's culture or what the government might do to the church, we should also take very seriously this threat of apostasy. We may mourn the decay of the world all around us, but the greatest danger to us is within our churches. Vance Havner, a preacher whose ministry influenced many people, wrote, "The temple of truth has never suffered so much from woodpeckers on the outside as from termites within."[4]

Back in January 1967, the Apollo space program suffered a terrible tragedy when astronauts Gus Grissom, Ed White, and Robert Chaffee were killed while doing some preflight checks in their space capsule. An electric spark triggered a fire that spread quickly in the oxygen-rich environment, and the men were unable to escape the capsule. Later, during some investigative hearings, when astronaut Frank Borman was asked about the root cause of the accident, he said it was a failure of imagination.[5] He pointed out that the space program had been preparing the astronauts for everything that could go wrong outside the capsule—the fires of reentry, the cold of outer space, and other external dangers. But no one had considered any possible threats inside the capsule.

Likewise, for the church, a failure to appreciate what can happen on the inside can get us in trouble. We're so fixated by what's happening outside that we're not paying attention to the inside. In Revelation 2:5, Jesus said to the church at Ephesus, "Repent...or else I will come to you quickly and remove your lampstand from its place." That applies to all churches. Christ is serious about the spiritual health of His church. If something is wrong, it can imperil the church.

Someone once put it this way: "The church's future lies not in reforming society, but in reforming itself." As 1 Peter 4:17 says, judgment should begin at the house of God. Only a repentant church can endure and win an unrepentant world. The enemy is working feverishly today in seminaries, churches, and ministries to pry people away from trusting in the inspired, living Word of God. The reason apostasy is so dangerous is that it's an inside job.

## THE DEFINITION OF APOSTASY

By this point you may be asking, "What exactly is apostasy?" Before we go any further, let me give a definition. Here is how pastor Andy Woods describes it:

> The English word apostasy is derived from two Greek words. The first word is the preposition *apo*, which means "away from." The second word is the verb *histēmi*, which means, "to stand." Thus, apostasy means, "to stand away from." Apostasy refers to a departure from known or previously embraced truth. The subject of apostasy has little to do with the condition of the unsaved world, which has always rejected divine truth and therefore has nothing

from which to depart. Rather, apostasy pertains to the
spiritual temperature within God's church.[6]

Apostasy has to do with people who profess to believe yet go on to
abandon the truth. They depart from the doctrinal truths of Scripture.

In the Bible, apostasy is both doctrinal and moral. It shows up
in belief and behavior, in creed and conduct, in profession and practice. That's because when people depart from their beliefs in doctrinal
truth, inevitably their behavior will follow. Another reason apostasy
happens is because people will engage in behavior that is not allowed
in Scripture. To justify that behavior, they then change their belief.
So belief will pull behavior with it, but behavior can also affect what
we believe. The two are inextricably tied together.

Scripture tells us that apostasy is one of the signs that the Lord's
coming is drawing near. It's a sign of the times. Jesus Himself addressed
this threat in the Olivet Discourse, a sermon He gave two days before
He was crucified. In this message, He gave a list of the signs that
would precede His return to earth.

At the beginning of the list, Jesus said, "Take heed that no one
deceives you" (Matthew 24:4). Later, He said, "Many false prophets will rise up and deceive many" (verse 11). He spoke again about
deception in verse 24, saying, "False christs and false prophets will
rise and show great signs and wonders to deceive." In this discourse,
Jesus warned against deception more than anything else.

There is no doubt that within professing Christendom today, the
voices of deception are proliferating. That's why we can say we live
in serious times.

## THE BIBLE'S DESCRIPTIONS OF APOSTASY

What does the Bible say about apostasy? I want to point out some
Scripture passages that can help us to better understand this threat.

The Bible is the lens through which we understand the truth, and it's important that we be able to recognize how the truth is being twisted today.

### 1 Timothy 4:1

Here, the apostle Paul wrote to Timothy, "The Spirit expressly says that in latter times some will depart from the faith, giving heed to deceiving spirits and doctrines of demons." This alerts us to the fact false doctrines come from deceitful spirits and doctrines of demons. What will these false doctrines do? They will cause some to "depart from the faith."

The context of this passage is the "latter times." So as we approach Christ's coming, we can expect to see more and more people fall away from the faith.

### 2 Timothy 3:1-5

You may be familiar with this passage. Paul wrote,

> Know this, that in the last days perilous times will come: For men will be lovers of themselves, lovers of money, boasters, proud, blasphemers, disobedient to parents, unthankful, unholy, unloving, unforgiving, slanderers, without self-control, brutal, despisers of good, traitors, headstrong, haughty, lovers of pleasure rather than lovers of God, having a form of godliness but denying its power. And from such people turn away!

Paul began by saying, "Know this." That can be translated, "Mark this," or "Don't miss this." Then he described what people will do during "the last days."

Some people wonder if we are living in those days now. The answer is yes, there is plenty of evidence for that. But how far along are we? Hebrews 1:1-2 says, "God, who at various times and in various ways spoke in time past to the fathers by the prophets, has in these last days spoken to us by His Son." This tells us the last days encompass the entire time between the first and second comings of Christ. But notice that in 2 Timothy 3:1, Paul was more specific. He said, "In the last days perilous times will come."

During the long era between Christ's first and second comings, there have been and will be seasons that are especially difficult. The Greek word translated "perilous" means "grievous, ugly, terrible." The only other time this word is used in the New Testament is in connection with the two demoniacs in Matthew 8:28. These demoniacs were wild, crazy, and violent. So 2 Timothy 3:1 is saying we can expect the times to worsen as the church age progresses.

In 2 Timothy 3:1-5, Paul listed 19 characteristics or conditions that will prevail during these perilous times. And he gave this important clue in verse 5: He said these people will have a form of godliness but deny its power. These characteristics and conditions will exist within professing Christianity, not outside. The world has always been wicked and evil. But here, Paul is warning about people who profess to know God yet in reality don't. They will exhibit these traits and engage in apostasy.

### 2 Timothy 3:13

Paul wrote, "Evil men and impostors will grow worse and worse, deceiving and being deceived." As we progress through the church age, things will worsen. They will spiral downward.

### 2 Timothy 4:3-4

A short while after Paul wrote about how all Scripture "is given by inspiration of God" (2 Timothy 3:16), he said, "The time will come when they will not endure sound doctrine, but according to their own desires, because they have itching ears, they will heap up for themselves teachers; and they will turn their ears away from the truth, and be turned aside to fables" (4:3-4).

That's what we see happening today. People have itching ears and are listening to teachers who tell them what they want to hear. And they are leaving Bible-teaching churches that proclaim truths they don't want to hear. Paul's use of the phrase "the time will come" tells us that apostasy will increase, and it is a sign of the end times.

### Jude 1-25

Immediately before the book of Revelation we come to the book of Jude—a short epistle with 25 verses. The theme of the entire book is apostasy and false teaching. Jude's purpose for writing was to exhort believers "to contend earnestly for the faith" (verse 3). He warned about "certain men [who] have crept in unnoticed...ungodly men, who turn the grace of our God into lewdness and deny the only God and our Lord Jesus Christ" (verse 4).

I have always thought it is interesting that Jude—which is all about apostasy—comes before Revelation, which describes the events of the tribulation. I don't think that's an accident. I believe the order of these books was divinely inspired. It's as if Jude is the front door or the foyer to Revelation. Jude highlights the conditions that will prevail within professing Christianity as we approach the end times.

## THE ANTIDOTE TO APOSTASY

Now that we have looked at Scripture's definition of apostasy, let's consider the antidote to apostasy.

After Paul described apostasy in 2 Timothy 3:1-5, he wrote this in verses 10-11: "But you have carefully followed my doctrine, manner of life, purpose, faith, longsuffering, love, perseverance, persecution, afflictions." By opening with the phrase "but you," Paul was making a contrast. A few verses earlier, he described the culture. But here, he explained how our character and conduct are to be different.

Moving on to verses 14-15, Paul wrote,

> Continue in the things which you have learned and been
> assured of, knowing from whom you have learned them,
> and that from childhood you have known the Holy
> Scriptures, which are able to make you wise for salvation
> through faith which is in Christ Jesus.

Continuing and growing in the Scriptures is the antidote to apostasy. Paul then concluded with this grand declaration: "All Scripture is given by inspiration of God, and is profitable for doctrine, for reproof, for correction, for instruction in righteousness, that the man of God may be complete, thoroughly equipped for every good work" (verses 16-17).

The Bible is the antidote to apostasy. That's why we need to keep it so central in our lives, our families, and our churches.

## THE CONFUSION CAUSED BY APOSTASY

In 2 Thessalonians 2, we see an interesting example of deception that led to much confusion. Paul had taught the Christians at the church in Thessalonica for only a few weeks before he had to leave. Afterward, the church received a counterfeit letter that was supposedly from Paul. The letter contradicted Paul's earlier teaching that the rapture would take place *before* the tribulation—and therefore, believers will not face the judgments of that seven-year period. The letter, however, said that the day of the Lord had already arrived, and that the tribulation was now here.

Upon reading this, the Christians in Thessalonica became upset. Now they were being told they would go *through* the tribulation and not raptured beforehand. That's why Paul wrote, "We ask you, not to be soon shaken in mind or troubled, either by spirit or by word or by letter, as if from us, as though the day of Christ had come" (verses 1-2). He said this to calm their fears.

Then Paul wrote, "Let no one deceive you by any means, for that Day will not come unless the falling away comes first" (verse 3). The day of the Lord—the tribulation—would not happen until the apostasy occurred. Not until then would "the man of sin [be] revealed" (verse 3). That refers to the antichrist. So the apostasy or falling away would occur *before* the tribulation. Because the apostasy hadn't happened yet, that meant the tribulation was not yet here.

There is one additional point to observe here. Some people believe the "falling away" in 2 Thessalonians 2:3 refers to the rapture because the word *apostasy* means "departure." They believe Paul was speaking of a physical departure, and not a spiritual one.

But there is a serious problem with that view. The Greek term *apostasia* refers to an active departure. It speaks of a person initiating the action. But that's not what will happen at the rapture. For us, the rapture will be a passive event. We won't be actively departing; rather, we will be passively "caught up" by the Lord. To say that the departure in 2 Thessalonians 2:3 is the rapture misrepresents what will actually happen at the rapture.

For this reason, we can know the apostasy in 1 Thessalonians 2:3 refers to a spiritual falling away and abandonment from the truth. For the sake of clarity, we can call this the Apostasy (with a capital *A*) because it refers to the great and final falling away. When that happens, then the man of lawlessness, or the antichrist, will be revealed, and the tribulation will come.

Theologian John Stott put it this way: "*The day of the Lord...*cannot be here already because *that day will not come* until two other things have happened. A certain event must take place, and a certain person must appear."[7] Stott calls the event the rebellion, and the person the man of lawlessness, or the rebel. Before the day of the Lord can come, there must be a rebellion and a rebel. Both are tied together because ultimately, the great apostasy will lead to all of the world worshipping the antichrist as God.

Some people think the great apostasy is already here. It is true that the church has always been afflicted by apostasy, but there is coming a greater and final apostasy. And I believe we are on the leading edge of it.

## THE SIGNIFICANCE OF TODAY'S APOSTASY

The great apostasy will be a sign that the end is approaching. You could say it is one of the runway lights that signal Jesus Christ is approaching soon. We're already seeing a growing tidal wave of apostasy today that is affecting many seminaries and entire denominations. It's also swallowing up churches. Someone once said, "The apostasy will take place and the churches will remain full." That's a sad commentary on what will happen.

In a book titled *Impossible People*, Os Guinness wrote this powerful statement: "Many churches have been lobotomized but carry on as if nothing has changed."[8] That's true, isn't it? Though churches are straying from Bible doctrine, they aren't doing anything about it. The apostasy we see happening today is taking us toward the full-blown and final falling away predicted in 2 Thessalonians 2:3.

There are some Christians today who believe a global revival could take place in the near future. While that is possible and we should pray for many to become saved, Scripture doesn't give any prophecies about a revival before the rapture. John Phillips offers this perspective:

> The river of apostasy is rising today. The "perilous times" of which Paul wrote are upon us. Soon the river will overflow its banks as all the tributaries of delusion and deception join the mainstream. When it reaches flood level, that river will inundate the earth in the final apostasy, which is the enthronement of the Devil's messiah as this world's god and king...Some think we can look for a worldwide

spiritual awakening before the Rapture of the church, but the passage in 2 Thessalonians indicates the opposite; a worldwide departure from the faith can be expected. God might indeed send a revival before He calls home the church, but the Scriptures do not prophesy one.[9]

Today, the Bible is under attack. Liberally minded people are chipping away at the foundation, doing damage to doctrinal truth and replacing it with what they want to hear. They are drifting away from the Bible as the final authority for doctrine and practice. And when the Bible is cast overboard and no longer our final authority, we end up drifting aimlessly on a sea of subjectivity.

## THE DAMAGE FROM TODAY'S APOSTASY

In my library, I have a book titled *The Last Week* by Marcus J. Borg and John Dominic Crossan. In the book, they go through the last week of Jesus' life. What's stunning is that they say it doesn't matter whether you believe in Jesus' resurrection. It's merely a parable, and we don't have to believe it happened.

But if they are correct, how do they deal with what Paul wrote in 1 Corinthians 15? "If Christ is not risen, then our preaching is empty and your faith is also empty…And if Christ is not risen, your faith is futile; you are still in your sins!…[and] we are of all men the most pitiable" (verses 14, 17, 19). Paul was saying that if Christ has not risen, then we are fools who believe in a lie.

Our salvation hinges on Christ's resurrection. If there is no resurrection, then how are we saved? Romans 10:9 says, "If you confess with your mouth the Lord Jesus and you believe in your heart that God has *raised Him from the dead*, you will be saved" (emphasis added).

And yet, there are people who claim it doesn't matter whether Jesus was raised. We don't have to believe He arose from the dead.

We are seeing an increase in the number of people who are chiseling away at the truths that salvation is through Jesus alone, and that He is the only way to God. They say, "Everyone can come to God their own way." But Jesus is the only way to heaven. All other ways lead to hell. People don't want to believe in hell, so they chisel away at that doctrine and discard it. They want to ignore it. But the reality of hell is not going away just because people refuse to believe in it.

This persistent chiseling away at foundational biblical truths is doing a lot of damage in other areas. For example, people have twisted what the Bible says about morality and marriage. When the US Supreme Court ruled on *Obergefell v. Hodges*, same-sex marriage was legalized nationwide. At the time, there were prominent professing Christians who couldn't line up fast enough to celebrate the court's decision. They included Tony Campolo, Rob Bell, Jen Hatmaker, Sarah Held Evans, and others.

More and more, people are saying that the Bible doesn't really mean what we've thought it meant for the past 2,000 years. They claim all of this is an epiphany, but I would suggest we're actually seeing expediency. They say they love God, but they want to be loved and embraced by the culture and don't want to swim upstream. The Bible makes it very clear that God designed for marriage to be between a man and a woman, as stated in Genesis 1:27-28. That's the marriage God created, and that's what He blesses—a heterosexual, monogamous marriage.

God made His views on homosexuality clear in Romans 1:26-32, 1 Corinthians 6:9-10, and 1 Timothy 1:9-10. One argument you will commonly hear from people is, "Jesus Himself never talked about homosexuality." But the Old Testament was already clear on the subject so Jesus didn't have to mention it specifically. Even so, in Matthew 19, when Jesus spoke against divorce, He said, "Have you not read that He who made them at the beginning 'made them male and female'…?" (verse 4). Here, Jesus quoted from Genesis 1:27, affirming that marriage is between a man and a woman. During His earthly ministry, Jesus also spoke about Sodom and Gomorrah—cities known for rampant homosexuality—in the context of judgment (Matthew 10:14-15; 11:23; Luke 17:29).

And it's gotten worse. We've gone beyond same-sex marriage to large numbers of gender identities. It's no longer just males and females. All of this has brought about massive confusion, and it's tragic. There are young people growing up in unstable homes and families, and they're caught up in this confusion. When it comes to morality and marriage, everything is now up for grabs. In a message based on Romans 1, titled "The Deepening Darkness," pastor Ray Stedman observed, "When men lose God, they always lose themselves."[10]

Those who promote the health and wealth gospel are also chiseling away at the foundations of biblical truth. Then there's the seeker-friendly movement, which waters down the gospel so people won't be offended by it. There's also what is called the gospel of self-fulfillment. The idea behind it is that God's love is so boundless that we don't need any boundaries on our choices. We can do whatever we want. Our goal should be to pursue happiness, and you sin only when you fail to reach your full potential. Self has replaced God on the throne—it gets to decide what's true and what isn't.

These ideas and others like them are infiltrating the church and Christianity. They are subtle and appealing, and they are couched in terms of acceptance, love, and open-mindedness. Those who dare to respond with biblical truth and the gospel are put on the defensive and shamed as if they were narrow-minded and unloving.

The book of Jude tells us that apostates will creep into the church unnoticed (verse 4). They don't come into the church with a name-tag that says, "Apostate riding on a broom." They do their work subtly, and people don't realize what is happening. It's interesting that Jude calls such apostates "clouds without water" (verse 12). As clouds, they appear to promise rain, but in reality, they are empty. They are deceiving.

What's happening in many churches today is that people are hearing the words *salvation* and *redemption*, but the preacher who is speaking those words means something very different from what the Bible means. Bait-and-switch is taking place, and to detect this, we need keen discernment.

## THE NECESSARY RESPONSES TO APOSTASY

### *A Modern-Day Reformation*

What we desperately need today is a modern reformation. The original reformation—which began with Martin Luther's posting of 95 theses on the door of the Castle Church in Wittenberg, Germany—was a Bible movement and a gospel movement. It dealt with the questions, Who is our authority—the Bible or the pope? And, How do we get to heaven—by God's grace alone through faith alone in Christ alone, or do we have to add human merit to God's grace?

The authority in our culture today is people's feelings, and we need to return to biblical authority. We need *sola scriptura*—Scripture alone—rather than the culture deciding what we should believe. One summer, my wife and I were traveling in Europe, and we went to the Reformation Wall in Geneva. It's a powerful historical landmark, and at the center are statues featuring William Farel, John Calvin, Theodore Beza, and John Knox. What struck me is that every one of them had a Bible under their arm.

The gospel taught in many churches today emphasizes human merit. But true salvation is apart from any human effort. It's by God's grace alone through faith alone in Christ alone. We don't dare be wrong about how to be right with God. There are many things we can be wrong about, but we cannot be wrong about the gospel, which means the difference between heaven and hell.

On the Reformation Wall, in Latin, are the words "After darkness, light." In the midst of spiritual darkness, light came through the Word of God and the gospel. But there are many in today's church who are changing that to "After light, darkness." They are going back to the darkness caused by not following the right authority and not teaching the true gospel.

### A Commitment to Christ and Conviction

So what are we to do? Here is what we need to see happen:

First, if you don't know Christ as your Savior, you need to be aware that Jesus is coming soon for those who have already come to Him. If you have never come to Him, He's not coming for you. What do you need to do? Romans 10:13 says, "Whoever calls on the name of the LORD shall be saved." All you have to do is call upon Him. Recognize that you are a sinner and ask Him to save you. He will wash away your sins and give you eternal life (1 John 1:9; Romans 6:23). Once you have come to the Lord Jesus Christ, you will have the assurance that someday, He's going to come for you.

Second, we need to preach and teach the Bible. Pastors and Bible study teachers need to simply preach and preach simply. All believers need to love the truth and get to know sound doctrine. We need to know what Scripture teaches and hold to those truths. When it comes to doctrine or morality, we're not to be innovative or novel. Pastor H.A. Ironside, the longtime pastor of The Moody Church in Chicago, was known for saying, "If it's new, it's not true, and if it's true, it's not new."

There's a story about Billy Graham that a critic once accused him of setting the church back 50 years because of his uncompromising commitment to the authority of God's Word. Upon hearing what the critic said, Graham jokingly responded, "I'm afraid I've failed. I was hoping to set the church back two thousand years!"[11] That's what we need to do—get back to the Scriptures and Jesus and the apostles, to the Word as it was given to us by God long ago.

We also need to pass the baton to the next generation. We are trustees of the truth and we are called to pass it on. Paul told Timothy in 2 Timothy 2:1, "The things that you have heard from me among many witnesses, commit these to faithful men who will be able to teach others also." Notice that there are four generations present in that one verse. There is no success without succession. You can have the fastest runners in the world on a relay team, and if they don't pass the baton correctly, the race is over. As the trustees of God's truth, it is essential for us—in our homes, in our churches, and through our ministries—that we reach the next generation. We must pass on the gospel, a precious treasure, and keep it intact.

Finally, Jude gave us this exhortation in verses 20-23:

> You, beloved, [be] building yourselves up on your most holy faith, praying in the Holy Spirit, keeping yourselves in the love of God, looking for the mercy of our Lord Jesus Christ unto eternal life. And on some have compassion, making a distinction, but others save with fear, pulling them out of the fire, hating even the garment defiled by the flesh.

We're to build ourselves up, and we're to reach out to others. We live in a day when people are filled with doubt and being defiled by what is happening all around us. We need to be on the lookout for those who need help. We're to have mercy on those who are struggling and, with proper fear, pull people away from the pollution caused by the flesh.

From there, the book of Jude closes with these powerful words:

> Now to Him who is able to keep you from stumbling,
> and to present you faultless
> before the presence of His glory with exceeding joy,
> to God our Savior,

who alone is wise,
be glory and majesty,
dominion and power,
both now and forever.
Amen (verses 24-25).

The dark and ominous book of Jude ends with a calm doxology that God is going to see us through to the end. "He who has begun a good work in you will complete it until the day of Jesus Christ" (Philippians 1:6).

We live in a decaying and dying world. And because the world is at its worst, the church needs to be at its best. We need to be at our best in our conduct, our character, and our creed so that we can effectively witness for Christ. After all, the church of Jesus Christ is the only hope for this world.

If we're compromising and corrupt, we will dilute and diminish the witness we have. We will be ineffective in fulfilling our calling. Only a repentant church can survive and win an unrepentant world.

## THE SACRED DUTY WE'VE BEEN GIVEN

If you've ever been to Washington, DC, chances are you're familiar with The Tomb of the Unknown Soldier. To me, this is one of the most gripping, most profound memorials among many others, and it's located at Arlington National Cemetery.

The tomb is guarded constantly 24 hours a day, 365 days a year. This has been going on since 1937. The changing of the guard takes place at the top of every hour from October 1 to March 31, and once every half hour from April 1 to September 30. This continues no matter what the weather, through every holiday, without fail.

On each shift, a single guard will walk 21 steps along a straight and narrow path near the tomb, stop, do a partial rotation for 21 seconds, then another partial rotation for another 21 seconds, then take 21 steps back along the path. This tribute is repeated nonstop through the entire shift. The guard's movements are crisp and executed to perfection. The significance of the number 21 is that it represents the 21-gun salute, which is the highest military honor that can be given to a soldier.

One of the most moving aspects of this rigorous watch takes place at the end of each shift, when a new guard reports for duty. The departing guard gives a simple order to the guard replacing him: "Post and orders, remain as directed."[12] At the end of every single shift, day in and day out, the order is passed on.

That's the challenge I want to issue here: The orders we have been given by our Master remain as directed. Nothing has changed.

What did Jesus say? "Go therefore and make disciples of all the nations, baptizing them in the name of the Father and of the Son and of the Holy Spirit, teaching them to observe all things that I have commanded you; and lo, I am with you always, even to the end of the age" (Matthew 28:19-20).

May we be found fulfilling those orders when our Lord Jesus comes. We can't stem the tide of all the apostasy that's taking place. We can't correct all the errors infiltrating the church. But we can follow the orders that our Master has given to us as we await His coming. We can be faithful to His calling to pass the baton on to the next generation, and to shine the light of God's Word into the darkness all around us.

# CHAPTER 10

# PROPHECY Q&A ROUNDTABLE

## JAN MARKELL, AMIR TSARFATI, JACK HIBBS, BARRY STAGNER

**Jan:** We live in interesting days. All around us, people are being deluded by falsehood. They listen only to what they want to hear. Deception is on the rise. Christ said that would happen as we draw closer to the end times. Incompetence is another serious problem—we're seeing a lot of that from those in positions of power.

How should the church behave today? How should those in the pulpit respond? And how can we as Christians counter these trends that are doing so much damage?

**Jack:** In Psalm 107:20, we read that God "sent His word and healed them, and delivered them from their destructions." In the New Testament, the apostle Paul wrote that "the church of the living God [is] the pillar and ground of the truth" (1 Timothy 3:15). Pastors need to either be in the Word of God more or get out. They need to step up or step out. This is not a time for spiritual weakness. We are at war against invisible forces. It's no longer cool or acceptable to be a Christian. The warfare around us is real and getting worse.

**Amir:** We should not be shocked by the delusions and deception around us. Scripture says that is exactly what will happen as we approach the end times. We are in those days. The fact Israel is standing alone more than ever and America is becoming weaker shouldn't surprise us. These things must take place. God is above time, and He already saw the future when He sent us an email with the book of Revelation attached to it. He said, "Here is what you can expect to happen. Trust Me, I've seen it."

The Bible also warns about the consequences of mankind's sinful nature. John 3:18 says, "He who believes in [Jesus] is not condemned, but he who does not believe is condemned already." To not be condemned is to believe in Jesus as the only way, truth, and life, and that no one comes to the Father but through Him (John 14:6). We are to proclaim the fact people are sinners, warn them about the wages of sin, explain the free gift of salvation, and help them learn how God wants us to live. The name of Jesus needs to be declared from pulpits more than anything else.

**Barry:** Peter said that "if you are reproached for the name of Christ, blessed are you" (1 Peter 4:14). The word "reproached" means "to be insulted" or "to be injured." We as a church need to recognize that when people disparage our faith, we have an opportunity to glorify God. Acts 5:41 said that when the apostles were beaten for proclaiming Christ, they rejoiced "that they were counted worthy to suffer shame for His name." This means the challenges we face as Christians should be viewed as opportunities.

Just as it wasn't safe to be a Christian in the first century, it's not always safe today. We've all seen the Christian fish symbol that appears on bumper stickers or T-shirts. That comes from the early church. The letters that often appear inside the fish are ICTHUS, an acrostic comprised of the first Greek letter in the words that translate to Jesus Christ, Son of God, Savior. The early Christians would draw this symbol to secretly indicate to other believers that they were followers of Christ. It was risky to be a believer in those days, and that's how Christians privately identified one another—all because they were persecuted for their faith.

We should never think we will be exempt from persecution. We are living in a time when we can expect to be criticized for our faith. And that gives us opportunities to bring glory to God by being faithful to Him in all that we say and do.

**Jan:** What are some ways we can recognize pastors and Christians who are becoming more progressive in their theology? For example, we know that in progressive Christianity, among the main buzzwords are *social justice* and *critical race theory*. What can we expect to hear from those who are becoming more woke in their teaching?

**Jack:** I'll start by saying progressive pastors don't talk about sin or repentance. You won't hear them mention the cross. They won't talk about sacrifice. Pastors who are progressive are not likely to teach from the Bible in an expository manner. They will skip the uncomfortable passages and chapters in the Bible. If you see a pastor skipping difficult portions of God's Word, that may be a sign he is progressive.

**Jan:** Progressive pastors will also show disdain for Bible prophecy, and they will never be a real friend to Israel. Amir travels to churches more than the rest of us, and I'd like for him to give us his perspective.

**Amir:** The more I have traveled and learned about what is happening in churches today, the more I've come to realize that when a church holds to wrong teachings about Israel, it will also hold to wrong teachings about other matters in the Bible. Israel is a litmus test for pastors and churches. That's also true about churches that fail to teach Bible prophecy.

In Luke 24, we read about the two disciples who were on their way to Emmaus. Keep in mind these were disciples, not Pharisees or Sadducees or Romans. They were sad because Jesus had been crucified. As they talked with one another, the risen Jesus approached them, and they didn't recognize Him. He asked them why they were sad, and they explained what had happened a few days earlier on the cross.

Then Jesus said, "Oh, foolish ones, and slow of heart to believe in all that the prophets have spoken!" The Lord rebuked these disciples because they hadn't understood the prophets, who said Jesus would come to suffer and die for their sins. They missed the whole point of God's plan of salvation and why the Messiah came. So Jesus read to them from the Scriptures and explained all that they said about Him. These disciples were confused because they hadn't paid attention to Bible prophecy.

I've noticed that when a church avoids talking about prophecy, it will not take a stand for Israel. In my opinion, that is a primary sign that a church has become progressive. If a church misses the point of Jesus' first coming in the same way the disciples did as they walked to Emmaus, they will not talk about Jesus' victory over sin. They won't present the gospel. The Lord Jesus Christ made it possible for us to be redeemed from sin, and He is coming back soon. That's the message we should proclaim.

**Barry:** When it comes to woke or progressive Christianity, I believe a good litmus test is this: If you're hearing more about how to improve your life and solve society's woes than you are hearing about the gospel and bringing people into the kingdom of God, then that's a warning, and you should leave.

**Jan:** There are many Christians who find themselves in this dilemma. Their pastor is a sound Bible teacher, and the message of salvation is being clearly proclaimed. But nothing is said about Christ's second coming or taking a stand with Israel. Is that a deal breaker even though the pulpit is sound? Should a believer stay in such a church?

**Jack:** Let me make one point clear before I give my answer. It is possible for Christians to differ on whether they hold to a pre-trib rapture view, or mid-trib or post-trib view because of how they were taught in their church or denomination. Many do not come to their conclusion on their own. They happen to hold to a particular view because of what they heard in their church. A person's position on the timing of the rapture doesn't mean the difference between going to heaven or hell. Scripture doesn't teach that.

However, I do not believe you can be a New Testament church and, at the same time, avoid Bible prophecy. To do so is to excise 27 to 30 percent of what is given to us in the Bible. The Holy Spirit would never do that. Revelation 19:10 tells us, "The testimony of Jesus is the spirit of prophecy." Jesus said He told us certain prophecies in advance so that when they happened, we would know who He is. God gave us Bible prophecy to reveal Himself to us. I don't see how a church that avoids Bible prophecy can be a New Testament church.

**Jan:** Amir, is a biblically sound pulpit that fails to address Bible prophecy a deal breaker?

**Amir:** I'm not a businessman, but let's put it this way: How often have you heard people say there is only one church they can go to in the area where they live? If that's the case, then I would say go there, and anything you're missing can be supplemented online or through other resources. Get involved in a church, but if the pastor isn't teaching Bible prophecy, find that teaching elsewhere. You don't want to say, "This church doesn't teach Bible prophecy, so I'm not going at all." You need Christian fellowship. That is important.

**Jan:** What do you say, Barry?

**Barry:** Many pastors are intimidated by Bible prophecy, but it's part of God's Word. As they teach through the Scriptures, they need to address prophecy whenever it comes up. They can't skip over the parts of God's Word that they think are too hard to understand or too difficult to address. When it comes to passages like Daniel chapters 7–8, pastors need to be willing to do a lot of study and homework so that they will understand the text clearly and can teach it to their church. Yes, it will take a lot of effort to teach from the more difficult parts of Scripture, but pastors should be willing to do that.

I agree with what Amir says about going to a church that has a sound pulpit yet doesn't teach Bible prophecy—do what you can to get supplemental teaching elsewhere. Both of us have traveled all over the world and constantly hear about churches not teaching Bible prophecy. This forces many people to rely on supplements from elsewhere. But there is no substitute for fellowship—that is necessary. Sometimes there is no other choice but to go to a biblically sound church and learn about Bible prophecy in other ways.

**Jack:** It is so important that the entire Bible be taught, including the 27 to 30 percent that is prophetic. One reason so many pastors aren't teaching prophecy is because the seminaries they attended don't offer any eschatology courses.

**Jan:** That is exactly right.

**Jack:** It's becoming more and more difficult for pastors to dodge their responsibility to teach Bible prophecy. We live in a world where people are looking for answers. They want to understand what is happening today, and that means they are going to ask questions about prophecy and the end times. Pastors can't keep avoiding that.

We must keep in mind that the very first word God gave in the Bible about the Messiah and salvation was a prophetic passage—Genesis 3:15. The first prophecy given in Scripture is about salvation from sin. You can't teach what this passage says about salvation and avoid the fact it is prophetic in nature. And that's true about many other passages—truths about salvation are often revealed in the context of prophecy. So when a pastor talks about salvation, there will be times he cannot avoid prophecy. A pastor is to teach all of what the Bible says.

**Jan:** That's a good point, Jack. That brings us to an extension of this question: What do you say to a believer or Bible teacher who simply isn't excited about Bible prophecy? What if they have no interest? What if they aren't paying attention to the fact we're living in the time of the signs and Jesus could return at any moment?

**Amir:** Hebrews 9:28 tells us about believers who "eagerly wait for Him," and the fact Jesus will "appear a second time." The first time He came, it was to bring salvation to the world, not judgment. Now we're to look forward to His return. Philippians 3:20 says those who are citizens of heaven "also eagerly wait for the Savior, the Lord Jesus Christ." In Titus 2:13, Paul adds to our attitude of eagerness a mandate for righteous and godly living as we look "for the blessed hope and glorious appearing of our great God and Savior Jesus Christ."

If we're not eager about Christ's soon appearance, we need to ask ourselves why. Scripture tells us we should live in expectation of His return. If that's not the case, then our understanding of Scripture is lacking.

Several years ago, I was asked to speak in Singapore. When I arrived at the airport, a deacon from a large church picked me up. He drove a beautiful car. "The Lord has blessed me so much," he said. "My business has prospered beyond measure. I make more money now than I've ever made my entire life. I am now building a house."

Then he said, "I don't mind if Jesus doesn't come back soon. I want to have time to enjoy my house."

This man loved his possessions more than he loved the coming appearance of Jesus.

There is only one time I have mercy for that kind of thinking—when I marry young couples. Before the wedding ceremony, I'll pray with the groom. In the prayer, I'll tell the Lord we look forward to His return. Often the groom will say, "Can Jesus wait just one more day?" I'll show mercy in that case.

But we should have the same attitude expressed by Paul in 2 Timothy 4:6-8: "I am already being poured out as a drink offering, and the time of my departure is at hand. I have fought the good fight, I have finished the race, I have kept the faith. Finally, there is laid up for me the crown of righteousness, which the Lord, the righteous Judge, will give to me on that Day, and not to me only but also *to all who have loved His appearing.*"

Paul makes it clear that we are to love the Lord's appearing.

**Jan:** Lately there's been a lot of talk about power shifts taking place in the world. As the United States's influence diminishes, the World Economic Forum and China are gaining more clout. These are among the new power players. But eventually, everyone's knee will bow to the antichrist. He will sweep the world off its feet. How will he do this? What can we expect to see happen?

**Amir:** I believe the world will experience such great chaos that everyone will welcome the antichrist and the peace he promises to bring. For a long time, the United States has been the policeman of the world. But what will happen when the US no longer fulfills that role?

Remove the US as the world's policeman, and every rat will come out of its hole. We're seeing North Korea pursue an aggressive nuclear weapons program. China is threatening all those who enter waters that are disputed territories and claiming those waters as its own. The Chinese military is also threatening Taiwan, the Philippines, and other neighbors in the Pacific. Those who disagree with what China is doing are afraid to speak up because they fear that will make matters worse.

Iran is carrying out attacks all over the Middle East through its terrorist proxies. Its nuclear weapons program continues to advance. Yet no one is holding Iran accountable. Russia and Turkey are friendly with Iran, and no one cares enough to stop Iran except Israel.

Scripture tells us that when the time comes for the Ezekiel 38–39 war to break out against Israel, no nations will come to Israel's aid. No one will help Israel to survive except for God Himself.

I also don't think China will become a world power. I believe China will face difficulties and become weaker, just like the US. That will be especially true when the rapture occurs and large numbers of Chinese Christians disappear. The resulting chaos will hurt China and contribute to its decline. And the antichrist will be too powerful for any nation to confront him.

**Barry:** We have to remember that the geopolitical landscape of the entire world will change during the tribulation. Daniel 11:39 says the antichrist will "divide the land for gain." Revelation 17:12 mentions ten kings who will rule with the antichrist and "have received no kingdom as yet." That tells us the antichrist is going to make geopolitical changes during his reign.

We also have to keep in mind that China is home to the underground church, which is massive. When the rapture happens, China is going to lose large numbers of people, and its governing authorities will be just as confused as other leaders around the world. In the middle of all the chaos, the antichrist will do a lot of smooth talking and deceive everyone into following him. We are going to see many changes take place rapidly.

**Jack:** Scripture says that the antichrist will deceive the world. He will promise peace and prosperity at a time when a lot is going wrong. There will be all kinds of mayhem, and very likely an economic collapse. The antichrist will see this as an opportunity to win people over by promising calm and stability.

**Amir:** Even during the first part of the tribulation, when the antichrist promises peace, depravity will be rampant. It will be so bad that the messages proclaimed by God's two witnesses will be considered blasphemous. When the witnesses are finally executed, people will celebrate. It will be like what happens after terrorist attacks in Israel, when Arab Muslims give candy to one another, and Jewish people line up to donate blood for the victims. That's the kind of hatred people will exhibit in the future. They will express contempt toward those who follow or represent God.

Moral standards will change radically. What we now consider good will be viewed as evil. And evil will be called good. When the antichrist rules the world, he will chop off the heads of those who refuse the mark of the beast. It won't be illegal for him to do that—the government will back him up. That's how bad the delusion will be.

**Jack:** Can we be clear that if you're a born-again believer, you won't see that because you'll be raptured before the tribulation?

**Jan:** Amen.

**Barry:** Scripture says that when God's two witnesses are killed, people will send gifts to one another all around the world. They will be glad the two Jewish prophets are dead (Revelation 11:10).

**Jan:** Moving on to another subject, what about the tyranny that took place in Australia during the COVID pandemic? The government cracked down severely on the people in that country. We also saw very prohibitive restrictions in the US, Canada, and Western Europe. Without any of us taking a stand on whether people should take the vaccine or not, it's been clear that governments used the vaccine as a tool to coerce people to the point that many of them were forced to leave their jobs. How should believers cope with such blatant tyranny?

**Barry:** What we've seen happen with government overreach is so troubling. After all, the government is responsible for protecting our rights, not our health. Our health is a matter we entrust to God. Yes, we should take advantage of the wonderful advances that have been made in medicine. But people should be allowed to make their own personal health decisions. When others violate that right, we should stand up.

Shortly after the church was born, the apostles were told not to preach in Jesus' name. They responded by saying, "Should we obey man, or God?" (see Acts 5:29). During COVID, some government authorities insisted that churches shouldn't meet. Yet Hebrews 10:25 says, we are "not [to be] forsaking the assembling of ourselves together, as is the manner of some, but exhorting one another, and so much the more as you see the Day approaching." That passage doesn't say, "Meet unless there is a pandemic." When authorities tell us that we can't obey God, we need to stand up against the tyranny.

Jack called attention to an article on social media that said certain groups of people were permitted to be exempt from the vaccine. This included the US Congress. The government was making different rules for different people.

**Jan:** So should we push back against this tyranny when it comes to our doorstep?

**Barry:** Isaiah 54:17 says that "no weapon formed against you shall prosper, and every tongue which rises against you in judgment you shall condemn. This is the heritage of the servants of the LORD, and their righteousness is from Me." So yes, we are to push back when the government tells us to do something contrary to what God says.

**Jack:** The apostle Paul told the Christians in Corinth they were to be "ready to punish all disobedience when your obedience is fulfilled" (2 Corinthians 10:6). We expose wickedness and punish disobedience by walking in the light with the Lord and making sure we're being obedient.

Proverbs 28:1 says, "The righteous are bold as a lion." So yes, we do push back. Now, in the city where our church is located, the local government and our county board of supervisors defended our right to exercise our faith. Why did they do that? Because we know them, and they know us. We pray for them and know them by name. Our church has ministry relationships with certain parts of the county. We help with chaplain supply and provide monetary support for emergency needs. So while we should stand against tyranny, we should also seek to be a positive influence on governing officials in our community.

**Jan:** Next, as we head toward the end times, could you summarize what we should be watching for in the Middle East? Amir, you're from Israel, and you've helped us to better understand the mess in the Middle East. What can you tell us?

**Amir:** When you talk about Bible prophecy, Israel becoming a nation again is a major development. It's the fig tree coming back to life (Matthew 24:32-33). So understanding what is happening in Israel and the Middle East is vital. Beyond that, we are seeing progress toward a one-world government, a one-world religion, and a one-world economy. The global platforms for these are being prepared now.

As for what is happening in the Middle East, we are witnessing developments no previous generation has ever seen. We are by far the most blessed generation since the time of Jesus because we are seeing more events of prophetic significance in our lifetime than those who lived over the past several hundred years. We are seeing things happen that the prophets wished they could see!

**Jack:** There are more developments we can mention. The United States is falling from its position as a superpower. The economy is in danger of collapsing, and the use of the dollar is declining worldwide. There are threats and rumors of wars. There's also the complete breakdown of the family. The LGBTQ agenda and gender identity issues are contributing to that. The Jewish people are back in the land of Israel, as prophesied in Ezekiel 36. And the stage is clearly being set for the Ezekiel 38 war. All these things are happening at the same time. Daniel prophesied that in the last days, "many shall run to and fro, and knowledge shall increase" (Daniel 12:4). Information will be transmitted and acquired at incredible speeds.

Never before have we seen so many prophetically significant trends and signs converge all at once. This is an ideal time for us to share the gospel with others. Many of the people around us are afraid. They may not show it, but they're terrified by what they see happening.

This means we need to set aside our pride and share the gospel. Let's be honest: A key reason many of us don't talk with our neighbors about Christ is because of pride. We don't want others to think we're crazy when we talk about Jesus Christ dying on the cross for their sins, then rising again from the grave.

Not only do we need to share the gospel, but we need to do so accurately. If you say, "Hey, do you believe in God?," your neighbor is likely to respond, "Of course I do." That's not sharing the gospel.

We shouldn't be afraid to talk with others about Jesus dying to take away their guilt and shame, and their need to repent of their sins. That's exactly what people need to hear. This is what people want—and need—to know. They want the assurance that when they die, they will enter Christ's presence. There are many who sense Jesus is coming back, and they are looking for answers.

**Jan:** Let's take time now to encourage our fellow believers with any closing thoughts you might have for them. Obviously, the greatest encouragement is the fact we are a privileged generation that is seeing many prophetic signs converge. Any day now, Jesus could come in the clouds to take us up to be with Him. What words of encouragement do you want to share?

**Barry:** I don't think there's anything more comforting or encouraging than to know that this life is not all there is. And that we're going to a place that words cannot adequately describe. We cannot imagine what awaits us. We will live in a place of unparalleled beauty and scope.

You may have heard the expression about people being so heavenly minded that they are no earthly good. But if you're heavenly minded, you're going to do *more* earthly good than normal because you're going to want to take people with you to heaven.

We have a mandate from God. I believe the great commission is established in the Old Testament in Proverbs 24:11-12: "Deliver those who are drawn toward death, and hold back those stumbling to the slaughter. If you say, 'Surely we did not know this,' does not He who weighs the heart consider it? He who keeps your soul, does He not know it? And will He not render to each man according to his deeds?"

We are here to save souls. That's our purpose. That's exciting, because "he who wins souls is wise" (Proverbs 11:30). We're here to act on behalf of the Lord. There isn't anything more thrilling in life than seeing someone's eternal destiny change. As long as we stay focused on our calling, we will be able to handle whatever the world throws our way. When you tell people about Jesus, you will have an exciting life.

**Amir:** When Jesus prepared to leave the disciples, He said we would do greater things than He did (John 14:12). What did He mean by that? Though Jesus healed blind people, those blind people still died. While Lazarus was resurrected by Jesus, he eventually died again. In contrast, God has given us the gospel to spread. The physical healings that Jesus offered were wonderful, but they were temporary. The spiritual healing that He brought through His death on the cross, however, is eternal. Obviously, we are not greater than Jesus. But He entrusted us with the most powerful means to bring change to planet Earth. When we share the good news, we are showing people the path to the spiritual healing Jesus offered. Our hearers are given the opportunity to repent of their sins, give themselves to the Lord Jesus, and receive the gift of eternal life.

Jesus wants to find us busy doing His work when He comes back. That's why we want to be diligent about sharing the gospel.

**Jack:** My encouragement is that you read the Gospels again. Do a fresh read through Matthew, Mark, Luke, and John, and ask yourself this simple question: What gave Jesus the greatest joy? You'll notice that Jesus rejoiced when people came to salvation. That is what brought a smile to Jesus' heart—to see people become saved.

To point others to the way of salvation should give us joy as well. Our greatest pleasure ought to be to share the good news with those around us.

# CHAPTER 11

# SATAN'S SUBTLE SCHEME TO SILENCE BIBLE PROPHECY

## JAN MARKELL

A t Olive Tree Ministries, we receive thousands of emails every month from people who ask all kinds of questions about Bible prophecy. The variety never ceases to amaze me. But there is one very difficult issue that comes up so frequently it breaks my heart. It's surprising how widespread the problem is, and it's sad that so many people have been hurt as a result. I believe you'll see what I mean after I share a few of these emails:

> My husband and I recently met with our church elders to ask why we never hear teachings about eschatology or the fact Israel is still God's chosen people. We were so disappointed to hear the elders say that Bible prophecy is divisive because people hold to so many different views about the end times, and therefore, they will never teach it. They said the most important thing is to present the gospel, and that's what they will stick with.

What are we to do? Stay and fight for all of God's truth to be taught, or find another church that is solid and teaches all of the Bible? Our hearts are heavy knowing that if we stay and continue to teach a complete and literal reading of God's Word, we will probably be asked to leave.

Another person wrote,

> I just read an article in your print newsletter about the remnant church, and I want to thank you for what you said. You hit the nail on the head—everything you mention, I am experiencing at my church. I feel so alone. No one wants to discuss the events of the day, and certainly not eschatology. When I mention these things, people shudder.

Still another wrote this:

> My husband and I are visiting churches. We have not found any that address the important issues of today and how they relate to the Bible. Some of the leaders we have met have gotten angry with us and asked that we not come back. I feel like crying when that happens. As I sit in the pew, I wonder why they never teach about what's happening in Israel and the intensity of the prophetic birth pangs our world is experiencing today.

Many of these Christians say they are lonely for like-minded believers. They want to understand Bible prophecy and the times in which we live. Prophetically, we are in one of the most significant eras in history, yet too many churches refuse to talk about prophecy even though so much of the Bible is devoted to it.

## THE DANGERS OF NOT
## TEACHING BIBLE PROPHECY

Why are so many churches reluctant to teach on Bible prophecy? There are a number of reasons. But no matter what they are, ultimately, we have to recognize that to avoid teaching Bible prophecy plays into Satan's subtle scheme to silence all things relating to eschatology.

Satan is glad when prophecy isn't taught. He doesn't want people to know how history will end for him. He doesn't want Christians to be motivated to live holy lives because Jesus might return soon. And he doesn't want unbelievers to feel any urgency about their need to come to salvation.

When a church's leaders avoid Bible prophecy, they end up making their congregation vulnerable to unbiblical ideas about eschatology. People are naturally curious about the future, and if they don't learn about it in their church, they may search for the answers in the wrong places. They may look to false or sensational teachers who appear to be biblical but aren't.

Even the secular world wants to know what the future holds. Psychics and horoscopes have always been in demand. But in recent decades, we've seen a new trend emerge. People are sensing that Earth is approaching its last days. A survey done by Pew Research in 2022 showed that nearly 40 percent of adults in the US believe we're "living in the end times."[1] A cover story on the November 1, 1999, issue of *Newsweek* was headlined "Prophecy: What the Bible Says About the End of the World." On June 29, 2014, *Time* magazine ran an article titled "What the Bible Really Says About the Rapture."

Unfortunately, when the secular media addresses Bible prophecy, usually people end up with incorrect information about what Scripture teaches. For example, on April 13, 2018, *USA Today* featured a short video titled "Biblical prophecy claims the rapture coming by month's end."[2] In this case, all *USA Today* did was pass along a prediction made by people who didn't know what they were talking about.

The *Daily Express* in the UK picked up the same story.[3] Those who are uninformed about Bible prophecy—both Christians and non-Christians—are susceptible to such deception. That's why it's so vital for churches to teach on Bible prophecy.

When Christians are left in the dark about prophecy, they can easily develop wrong perceptions. They may assume that Jesus isn't coming back. Or, they may think, *Come, Lord Jesus, but not too soon. I'm enjoying life on earth too much right now.* These mindsets are unfortunate because Jesus Himself warned, "Watch therefore, for you do not know what hour your Lord is coming" (Matthew 24:42).

These are among the reasons it's so important for churches to teach eschatology. And here are two more: God's love for us compelled Him to inform us about the future. That's why He made more than one-fourth of the Bible prophetic at the time it was written. Also, God loves His chosen people and has plans for them. In the Bible, He has revealed a lot to us about Israel's past, present, and future, and He wants us to be excited about what He has done and will do. When a church doesn't teach about Israel, Satan is happy because Satan hates what God loves.

## THE REASONS BIBLE PROPHECY IS SO ESSENTIAL

In 2 Peter 1:19-20, we are given this exhortation: "We have the prophetic word confirmed, which you do well to heed as a light that shines in a dark place." That's what Bible prophecy is—a lamp shining into the darkness. I've often said that we would go out of our minds without this light, for it is God's promises about the future that help to quiet our hearts and give us hope.

As 1 Corinthians 2:9 says, "Eye has not seen, nor ear heard, nor have entered into the heart of man the things which God has prepared for those who love Him." This talks about the future God has in store for believers—a future that is glorious. But for unbelievers, the future is big trouble. If churches aren't teaching Bible prophecy, both believers and unbelievers are left unaware of what is to come. We can correctly say that eschatology is God's way of giving people warnings about the future in advance. God has given us this information for reasons that matter.

There is much that Christians can learn from the topics of prophecy and Israel. We could list many ways that we benefit from learning about these subjects, but here are some significant truths to begin with:

- God keeps His promises
- He is a miracle worker
- He is in control even as the world seems to spin out of control
- We are reminded that God has special plans for Israel and Christians
- We are called to live with an eternal perspective

In a world filled with so much confusion, it's easy to get discouraged. As we endure trials, heartaches, and difficulties, we become distressed and wonder how much more we can take. But when we are reminded that there is coming a day when we will be raptured, we are encouraged. Prophecy helps us to look past our troubles and look to the wonderful future ahead of us.

Bible prophecy is meant to encourage us with the assurance that Jesus is coming, He will deliver us, and He will judge this world. Back in the days before the worldwide flood, God told Noah, "I'm bringing an end to all of this." God was grieved because man was so wicked "that every intent of the thoughts of his heart was only evil continually" (Genesis 6:5). Sin couldn't have gotten any worse. Jesus warned this will happen again in the end times: "As the days of Noah were, so also will the coming of the Son of Man be" (Matthew 24:37).

But God has promised He will bring judgment again and make this world right. That is the hope prophecy offers to us!

## THE REASONS BIBLE PROPHECY
## ISN'T BEING TAUGHT

Why is it that pastors and teachers don't want to deal with Bible prophecy? We're going to look at a few key reasons that I've modified from a list created by pastor Tom Hughes:[4]

1. *Pastors are not learning about eschatology in seminary.* Many Bible schools have dropped prophecy from their curriculum. Among those that do still teach eschatology, some are pushing unbiblical views, such as amillennialism or preterism or Kingdom Now theology.[5]

2. *Churches are afraid of offending people or scaring them off.* They fear that teaching Bible prophecy will cause people to leave. But that's a wrong perspective to have when God gave Bible prophecy to prepare us for the future and to give us hope. Yes, the judgments in the book of Revelation are frightening. But as we see God's wrath in action, we see that He is a God of justice and righteousness. We can learn important truths about God even in the difficult prophetic passages in the Bible.

3. *People might not tithe if they think we're near the end.* That may surprise you, but it's one of the reasons that appears on Tom's list. This is sad, but true. Pastors don't want to stand behind the pulpit and say, "The Lord could come back at any time" for fear that their congregations will no longer be motivated to give financially. They don't want to talk about Christ's soon return when there's a building program or other projects to raise money for.

4. *Churches are ashamed of the loony fringe in the world of eschatology.* You can't blame churches for this. There are too many people who have made wild claims about the future that have not come true. Date setters like Harold Camping and Edgar Whisenant repeatedly made incorrect predictions about Christ's return. Whisenant wrote a book titled *88 Reasons Why the Rapture Will Be in 1988*. When he was proven wrong, he revised his calculations—and was wrong again. These kinds of failed predictions are widely mocked by the media and are a huge embarrassment to the church. This is one of the reasons there are so many scoffers who say, "Where is the promise of His coming?" (2 Peter 3:4).

## THE ATTACKS ON BIBLE PROPHECY FROM WITHIN THE CHURCH

Another problem faced by those of us who love God's prophetic Word is teachers within the church who attack what we say about the end times. For example, speaker and author Rob Bell said,

> I would argue that in the last couple hundred years, disconnection has been the dominant way people have understood reality. And the Church has contributed to that disconnection by preaching horrible messages about being left behind and that this place is going to burn—absolutely toxic messages that are against the teachings of Scripture...[6]

I'm not sure how you can look at what the Bible teaches about the rapture and the future destruction of the earth and accuse those passages of being toxic. Yes, people will be left behind when Christ takes the church up in the rapture. And yes, God's wrath will be poured out on the world during the tribulation. But just because certain teachings in the Bible have a hard edge to them doesn't mean they are toxic.

Hank Hanegraaff, host of the *Bible Answer Man* radio broadcast, has repeatedly criticized the pre-trib view of the rapture on his program. In one episode, a questioner asked, "What I'm trying to understand is where do they get to teaching that the church will be raptured out, and will not have to go through [the] tribulation? Where is that found at?" Hanegraaff responded,

> It's not found. That's the whole point. The point is it's something that is imposed on the Scripture. The notion is a very new notion in church history. It's a nineteenth-century notion that was popularized by John Nelson Darby, and it comes with the presupposition that God has two distinct people. And therefore, He has two distinct plans for the two distinct people. And He has two distinct phases of the second coming and two distinct destinies. This, however, is an imposition on Scripture.[7]

Hanegraaff not only denies the pre-trib rapture but believes the idea of a pre-trib rapture is new in church history when, in fact, people wrote about the pre-trib rapture long before John Nelson Darby.[8] Hanegraaff is also a preterist,[9] which means he believes many of the prophecies in the book of Revelation were fulfilled in the past, in AD 70.

When key teachings about the end times are altered or denied, people are left confused and uninformed. That's what Satan wants. He is pleased when Scripture's warnings about Christ's return and God's future wrath are silenced or ignored. Unbelievers are robbed of the warnings about God's coming judgment, and believers are robbed of the hope God desires for them to possess in seemingly hopeless times.

## THE BENEFITS OF TEACHING BIBLE PROPHECY

Bible prophecy also encourages believers to have an eternal mindset in this temporary world. But when churches don't teach prophecy, people will lack that perspective. And they will become vulnerable to the prosperity teachers who say God wants us to live our best life now. When people become focused on living for today, they won't have their eyes on the future. They won't set their mind on things above instead of things on the earth (see Colossians 3:23).

Hebrews 10:24-25 stresses the importance of believers living with an awareness of Christ's coming. We are commanded to "consider one another in order to stir up love and good works, not forsaking the assembling of ourselves together, as is the manner of some, but exhorting one another, and so much the more as you see the Day approaching." The words "so much more as you see the Day approaching" communicate urgency. We're to exhort and encourage one another as our Lord's return draws nearer, for Christ could come at any time.

Revelation 1:3 promises a blessing to those who read the prophetic truths in the book of Revelation: "Blessed is he who reads and those who hear the words of this prophecy, and keep those things which are written in it, for the time is near." Any teacher who withholds Bible prophecy from other Christians also withholds blessing.

Second Timothy 4:8 says that a crown awaits those who love Christ's appearing. Paul wrote, "There is laid up for me the crown of righteousness, which the Lord, the righteous Judge, will give to me on that Day, and not to me only but also to all who have loved His appearing." Churches are to get people excited about Christ's coming so that they can receive this crown of righteousness.

It's only when we understand what the Bible teaches about Israel that we are able to fulfill the command given in Psalm 102:13: "You will arise and have mercy on Zion; for the time to favor her, yes, the set time has come." Zion refers to Israel, and this is a call to show mercy and favor to her. What we don't know is whether "the set time has come." Does that speak of when Israel became a nation in 1948? Does it refer to Israel during the millennium, when all of God's promises to Israel are fulfilled at last? Or is it right now? It could be any or all of those—we're not sure. But if we've been called to be gracious to Zion, then we shouldn't ignore what Bible prophecy says about Israel or be dismissive toward the Jewish nation.

One very important truth Bible prophecy teaches us is that God keeps His promises. He is a covenant maker and a covenant keeper, and the covenants He made long ago with Israel still stand. The fact He keeps His promises to Israel means He will also keep His promises to us. God's enduring care for Israel serves as a powerful confirmation that His care for us will never cease.

It is because God has kept His promises to Israel that the land formerly made up of swamps and deserts has become one of the most powerful countries in the world. At the time of this writing, Israel is ranked number 11 globally.[10] Israel's meteoric rise as a nation began a relatively short time ago, in 1948. Even Theodor Herzl—who during the 1890s played a critical role in helping spread the vision to reestablish the nation of Israel—probably never envisioned how successful Israel would become. It is God who made that possible, which gives us more reason to be diligent and learn what Bible prophecy teaches about Israel.

## THE RESISTANCE TO WHAT PROPHECY SAYS ABOUT ISRAEL

Israel's miraculous rebirth and growth has faced great opposition. The Arab nations surrounding the Jewish state have gone to war against Israel multiple times. World leaders and the United Nations have been highly critical of Israel. Antisemitism has been persistent, and since 2005, the Boycott, Divestment, Sanctions (BDS) movement has tried to cause economic and political harm to Israel. These are just some of the ways people have tried to stop Israel, but they won't succeed because they can't keep God from fulfilling His promises to Israel.

Satan has always wanted to stamp out Israel. Ever since God promised in Genesis 3:15 that the offspring of the woman would crush Satan's head, the devil knew he had to wipe out the Jews so that God's plans through the Messiah couldn't be fulfilled. Who would have ever thought that part of Satan's plan would include getting the church to be silent? And getting teachers to promote theologies that marginalize and reject Israel? These are part of Satan's subtle scheme today. For him, getting rid of Israel is a matter of self-preservation. He knows that as long as Israel exists, God's plans for the present and future will be fulfilled—plans that mean Satan's defeat is sure and eternal.

## THE DAMAGING EFFECTS OF REPLACEMENT THEOLOGY

One of the most damaging theologies against Bible prophecy and Israel is replacement theology, which teaches that in God's divine plan for the ages, Israel has been replaced by the church. This view says, "Israel's sin and failure caused God to set aside national Israel completely and permanently and replace it with the church. The promises given to Israel in the Old Testament have been transferred over to the church."[11]

The church father Augustine (AD 354–430) was among the earliest proponents of this view, which is taught today in many mainline Protestant denominations and the Catholic Church. In recent decades, a growing number of evangelical Christians have embraced replacement theology. But to teach this view is to say God didn't keep the unconditional covenant He made with Abraham in Genesis 15—a covenant that God alone took upon Himself to fulfill. Abraham was asleep as God walked between the animal pieces, which tells us Abraham—and therefore Israel—wasn't responsible for keeping this covenant. Therefore, Israel's disobedience could not cancel God's promise. While God has chastised the people of Israel, Romans 11:2 emphatically declares that "God has not cast away His people." The fact Paul wrote Romans 11:2 long after the crucifixion and resurrection is evidence that God's plans for Israel did not change when the people rejected their Messiah.

Another problem with replacement theology is how it allegorizes Bible prophecies rather than interpreting them literally. For example, rather than teach that Christ will rule over a literal kingdom here on earth for 1,000 years, proponents of replacement theology advocate amillennialism, which says there will be no literal, future kingdom. They say Christ's kingdom is already here spiritually. But to approach Bible prophecy allegorically is dangerous because it allows people to interpret prophetic passages any way they want.

Amillennialism also leaves no place for God to fulfill His future promises to Israel. All the Bible passages that talk about a literal future kingdom in which Christ rules from His throne in Jerusalem are disregarded and reinterpreted.

However, Zechariah 14 clearly talks about a future time when Jesus will rule from Jerusalem and "all the nations...shall go up from year to year to worship the King" (verse 16). In that day, "the LORD shall be King over all the earth" (verse 9). God tells us what will happen when Jesus rules from Israel: "Ten men from every language of the nations shall grasp the sleeve of a Jewish man, saying, 'Let us go with you, for we have heard that God is with you'" (Zechariah 8:23).

Those are just a few of the Bible's many prophecies about Christ's future literal kingdom, which will be based in Israel. Amillennialism does away with all that. It rejects the truth that God's kingdom promises to Israel will be fulfilled literally. It gives all those promises to the church and spiritualizes them. In doing this, replacement theology twists and diminishes Bible prophecy and Israel.

What's tragic is these attacks are coming from within Christianity, and they are having a detrimental effect on how the church views Israel. So it's not surprising that evangelical support for Israel has been declining, especially among millennials. The drop has been especially sharp in recent years. The Center for the Study of the United States (CSUS), which is based at Tel Aviv University, determined that "as of late 2021, only 33% of young Evangelicals under 30 support Israel, compared to 67.9% in 2018."[12] That's a decline of more than 50 percent in three years.

Dr. Yoav Fromer, the head of CSUS, pointed out the obvious implications of this: "Now, as younger generations of Evangelicals appear to be turning away, Israel must seek to cultivate new sources of popular support…If they don't do this, and fast, in 10-20 years when Israel finds itself in need of emergency American aid, there might not be anyone there to offer it."[13] Fromer is correct—this trend makes it clear future US policy toward Israel will be affected.

## THE EVIDENCE ISRAEL IS STILL PART OF GOD'S PLANS

One reason we know Israel is still an active part of God's plans for today and the future is because the primary purpose of the tribulation is for God to deal with the Jewish people. That's why Jeremiah 30:7 calls this seven-year period "the time of Jacob's trouble." Jacob represents Israel, and God will use this time span to get His people's attention and call them to Himself.

One key aspect of the tribulation is that a Jewish temple will once again stand on the Temple Mount. We know this because during the tribulation, the antichrist will commit what is called "the abomination of desolation" (Matthew 24:15). Christ warned that when this happens, the Jewish people are to flee (verses 16-20). Second Thessalonians 2:3-4 tells us exactly what this abomination will be: The man of sin—that is, the antichrist—will exalt himself by entering the temple and declaring himself to be God.

Still another Jewish element of the tribulation will be the 144,000 Jewish evangelists whom God appoints to proclaim the gospel to the entire world (Revelation 7:4-8). The Lord will choose 12,000 Jewish men from each of the 12 tribes of Israel. And the result of their ministry is described in verse 9, where we read about "a great multitude which no one could number, of all nations, tribes, peoples, and tongues, standing before the throne and before the Lamb." These are the tribulation saints—Christians who will be killed for their faith. They will have become saved because of the 144,000 Jewish messengers who declare the gospel.

God says that at the end of the tribulation, "I will pour on the house of David and on the inhabitants of Jerusalem the Spirit of grace and supplication; then they will look on Me whom they pierced. Yes, they will mourn for Him as one mourns for his only son" (Zechariah 12:10). God will bring about a mourning that leads to repentance among His people. As Paul says in Romans 11:25-26, the "blindness in part" that happened to Israel in the past will be lifted, and "all Israel will be saved."

Are you seeing how much the tribulation has to do with Israel? All through this time of wrath, God will be at work among His chosen people. And after Christ returns, He will establish His throne in Jerusalem. Zechariah 14:4 says, "In that day His feet will stand on the Mount of Olives." And from that point onward, Christ will rule from Israel as "King over all the earth" (verse 9).

All through history, Satan has wanted to prevent this from happening. He figured that if he could wipe out the Jews, he could thwart God's plan for the ages. That's always been his goal: to destroy the Jews. That explains the constant persecution of the Jewish people all through history—from the Pharaoh to the captivities to the Roman destruction in AD 70 to the inquisitions to the pogroms to the Holocaust to today. Satan has always wanted to get rid of the Jews.

And for the church to be silent about Bible prophecy and Israel only plays into Satan's scheme. He doesn't want Christians to understand God's plans. When believers are ignorant, they won't support Israel. Nor will they sense any urgency about the nearness of Christ's coming.

God's love for Israel is eternal. Zechariah 2:8 tells us Israel is the apple of God's eye. The promise He made in Genesis 12:3 has not changed. God said He would bless those who bless Israel, and that is still true today. In Jeremiah 31:35-36, God said Israel will not go away until the fixed order of the universe departs. As long as the heavenly bodies continue on their God-ordained paths, Israel will not cease to be a nation.

Since 1948, Israel has been a nation again. And during the millennial kingdom, our Lord will rule from Israel. At the second coming, Christ will descend to the Mount of Olives, and He will establish His throne in Jerusalem—not in Washington, DC, nor Paris, nor Rome, nor Cairo, nor Oslo, but Jerusalem.

## THE NEEDED MESSAGE OF BIBLE PROPHECY

Have you ever thought about how odd it is that God would choose the Jewish people and keep His promises to them, yet Christians would spurn them? That doesn't make sense apart from Satan wanting to do all he can to hurt Israel. And if God were to break His promises with Israel, that would mean He could break His promises to us too. Yet we know God will never do that to the Jewish people, nor to Christians. He keeps His promises—all of them.

This is why it is so necessary for pastors and churches to teach Bible prophecy. Seeing how God deals with Israel and understanding His plans for the future helps to build our faith. We are encouraged as we see that God is faithful to His promises: God *will* continue to extend His grace to Israel. Jesus *will* return. Judgment *will* come. Jesus *will* rule from Jerusalem.

First Peter 3:15 tells us to "always be ready to give a defense to everyone who asks you a reason for the hope that is in you, with meekness and fear." A big part of the hope we have comes from the assurance that Christ will return. We should never stop talking about "the blessed hope and glorious appearing of our great God and Savior Jesus Christ" (Titus 2:13).

We have a message people need to hear. Everything is falling into place for God's plans to be fulfilled. Christ is coming, and time is getting short. We want everyone—believers and unbelievers—to be ready for the arrival of the King of kings and Lord of lords.

# CHAPTER 12

# GOD'S PROPHETIC PULPIT IN THE LAST DAYS

### JACK HIBBS

In Revelation chapters 2–3, we read letters that Jesus wrote to seven churches in Asia Minor. In these letters, our Lord spoke not only to actual people and churches of that day, but also to churches for all time. What Jesus says here is just as relevant to us as it was for them.

The letter Jesus wrote to the church at Philadelphia stands out from the others because it doesn't include any rebukes, as most of the letters did. As you read what Jesus said, notice what He commended the church for:

> To the angel of the church in Philadelphia write,
>
> "These things says He who is holy, He who is true, 'He who has the key of David, He who opens and no one shuts, and shuts and no one opens': 'I know your works. See, I have set before you an open door, and no one can shut it; for you have a little strength, have kept My word, and have not denied My name. Indeed I will make those of the

synagogue of Satan, who say they are Jews and are not, but lie—indeed I will make them come and worship before your feet, and to know that I have loved you. Because you have kept My command to persevere, I also will keep you from the hour of trial which shall come upon the whole world, to test those who dwell on the earth. Behold, I am coming quickly! Hold fast what you have, that no one may take your crown. He who overcomes, I will make him a pillar in the temple of My God, and he shall go out no more. I will write on him the name of My God and the name of the city of My God, the New Jerusalem, which comes down out of heaven from My God. And I will write on him My new name.

'He who has an ear, let him hear what the Spirit says to the churches'" (Revelation 3:7-13).

Jesus recognized this church's works, and He praised these believers for keeping His Word and not denying His name. He loved these people and extolled them for persevering for His sake. He promised to deliver them and urged them to "hold fast."

What made this church so exceptional? We can be sure a biblically committed pulpit contributed to making this a biblically committed church.

Through the years, I've had many people approach me and say they have given up on trying to find a church that adheres to God's Word. So many churches no longer do that, which is tragic.

That's true about many churches in Southern California, where I live. But I wouldn't want to live in any other place for this one reason: In California, there is no gray area in which Christians can hide. You are either following Jesus Christ or you are not. I'm grateful that line has been drawn in the sand. Either you're committed or you are not.

Notice that Jesus opened in Revelation 3:7 by addressing the letter to the "angel of the church in Philadelphia." This isn't an angel with wings who oversees the church in a spiritual sense. The Greek term translated "angel" can be rendered "messenger," which tells us the letter is addressed to the pastor of the church, who bears the responsibility of passing God's Word on to the people. We can also say that a key reason Jesus wrote to the pastors of the seven churches is because the nature of a pastor's ministry is evident in the faithfulness—or lack of faithfulness—displayed by his church. That's a sobering reality.

With that in mind, I'd like for us to look at seven qualities a church's pulpit should have as we enter the last days. These qualities will apply to you even if you're not a pastor. That's because God works through all of us. And my hope is that you're eager to be a positive influence for change both within your church and outside of it. All of us should desire to be on fire in our service for the Lord these days.

## AN AUTHENTIC PULPIT

First, God's prophetic pulpit in these last days should be authentic. It needs to be a pulpit God can use.

The greatest doctrine that graces the chapters of the Bible is the doctrine of salvation. God's first-ever prophetic announcement in Scripture was that He would save people from their sins. In Genesis 3:15, He told Adam and Eve about a future Savior who would redeem them from their sins. That truth is repeated all through the Bible, and it's the number one message to proclaim from the pulpit today—that Jesus Christ alone saves. He is the way, the truth, and the life, and no one comes to the Father but through Him (John 14:6). We should declare that without apology.

That's what I mean when I say the pulpit needs to be authentic. Our focus should be to preach the gospel clearly.

What is the gospel? There is no salvation without stating the first word of the gospel message: *repent*. People need to repent and believe on the Lord Jesus Christ to be saved (Romans 10:9). The Greek word translated "repent" is *metanoia*, which means "to change your mind"— to change the way you think about Jesus Christ and turn from sin.

A.W. Tozer wrote,

> There is today no lack of Bible teachers to set forth correctly the principles of the doctrines of Christ, but too many of these seem satisfied to teach fundamentals of the faith year after year, strangely unaware that there is in their ministry no manifest Presence, nor anything unusual in their personal lives. They minister constantly to believers who feel within their breasts a longing which their teaching simply does not satisfy.
>
> I trust I speak in charity, but the lack in our pulpits is real. Milton's terrible sentence applies to our day as accurately as it did to his: "The hungry sheep look up, and are not fed." It is a solemn thing, and no small scandal in the Kingdom to see God's children starving while actually seated at the Father's table.[1]

What prophetic words from Tozer—you can be in a church yet starving and dying.

The pulpit cannot be authentic if the pastor who speaks from it is preoccupied with popularity or attention. A ministry cannot be judged by the pastor's charisma. For a pulpit to be authentic, it must honor Christ. It must be faithful to keep our Lord's Word and not deny His name. It must stand true even when persecution comes, as it will in these last days.

This authenticity must come not only from the pastor, but from everyone in the church. We all need to stand for Jesus and be true to the Word. No matter what our role as a Christian worker, we're to be authentic to the gospel. And that includes a willingness to be hated.

Here's the irony: Jesus Christ is the most loving individual who ever lived. Yet He is the most hated today.

In Jeremiah 3:15, God said, "I will give you shepherds according to My heart, who will feed you with knowledge and understanding." Does your church feed you with knowledge and understanding that is applicable so you can live an authentic Christianity?

This brings up a sobering truth: A shepherd has a significant influence on the sheep. Another way of saying this is that sheep are inclined to imitate their shepherd. And it's because of a lack of authentic pulpits today that we're experiencing a drought of authentic believers.

Jesus made it clear that shepherds are accountable for how they care for the Lord's sheep. In John 21, Jesus asked Peter three times, "Do you love Me?" (verses 15-17). Every time, when Peter said yes, Jesus responded, "Feed My sheep" (verse 17, see also verses 15-16). This was Jesus' test to Peter. A shepherd shows his love for Jesus by properly feeding the sheep who are in his care.

Your church should be the most dynamic and influential group of people in your community. Unbelievers should either be drawn to your church or terrified by it, and I mean that in a good way. They should be attracted to the gospel, and they should be aware that your church will take a stand for what is good and right and beneficial for your community.

In early America, along the east coast, cities were not laid out in neat, perfect grids like they are in the western states. Instead, roads went all different directions. But frequently, they led to a central point in town. They would often lead to a hub where a church was located. Churches were at the center of life in those days. People understood that God was central in their lives and that they answered to Him. Today, our influence should be such that people realize their need for God.

## AN ENGAGING PULPIT

What do I mean by having an engaging pulpit? There are too many churches today that don't want to get involved in the culture around them. They say, "We're not going to take a stand. We're just going to preach the gospel."

But a church cannot say it preaches the full counsel of God if it's not engaging with cultural issues and providing a biblical response to them. It's vital for churches to know how to address worldly matters from a biblical perspective.

Have you noticed how the culture is constantly engaging Christians? Secular society is actively pushing its godless views on our children and community. The prince of darkness is spreading his kingdom, and he is doing it by getting the culture to pressure Christians to be silent. For example, on the abortion issue, it's about killing babies. What's the consequence if the church doesn't speak up? When a church doesn't engage, that's a win for Satan.

God is calling for us to make our voice heard. And the pulpit must be at the tip of the spear when it comes to engaging with the culture. The pulpit must engage, and those in the church must follow their pastor's lead. This isn't simply politics; it is standing up for righteousness.

Yes, we are to preach the gospel, but after we do that, what comes next? Our biblical worldview should influence how we live. It should prompt us to action. After we've listened to the Word on the first day of the week, what are we to do the other six days? Live out what we've learned.

In Matthew 5:13, Jesus said, "You are the salt of the earth; but if the salt loses its flavor, how shall it be seasoned?" That last word means "re-seasoned." You can't re-season salt. Once it loses its flavor, "it is then good for nothing but to be thrown out and trampled underfoot by men."

Let's move back a bit to verses 10-12. How did Jesus set up His statement that we are to be "the salt of the earth"? He said, "Blessed are those who are persecuted for righteousness' sake, for theirs is the kingdom of heaven. Blessed are you when they revile and persecute you, and say all kinds of evil against you falsely for My sake. Rejoice and be exceedingly glad, for great is your reward in heaven, for so they persecuted the prophets who were before you."

Persecution is a given. We can expect it. We need to stand strong and speak the truth in love, no matter how difficult the circumstance. Make the gospel known and don't be afraid to engage with others. I believe strongly that the government and the culture cannot stop the church.

Some pastors are concerned about how the government might respond when their church engages the culture. They say, for example, "We don't want to lose our 501(c)(3) status." That is, their tax-exempt status.

But it's not worshipful to let concerns about a church's tax-exempt status hinder it from being authentic and engaging. To do that is to let the government dictate what the church does.

Governments in other countries have tried to silence the church, and they haven't been successful. A prime example is China, which has one of the fastest-growing Christian populations on earth. Russia has tried and failed. North Korea has media blackouts and severe restrictions on its people, yet there are thousands of Christians there. Governments cannot stop God; He is the God of governments (Isaiah 9:6).

Will governments ever be able to stop prayer? They can't. People are going to pray. Can political leaders keep people from reading the Bible? People will read God's Word even when it's illegal to do so.

The church shouldn't run and hide. It needs to engage the culture. Some years ago, Greg Laurie was featured on a banner about one of his upcoming Harvest Crusades. In the picture on the banner, he was holding up a Bible. He was attacked for that.

Greg texted me and said, "Did you see this?" I texted to him, "Use this as an opportunity. At the crusade, encourage all 50,000 people to stand and hold up their Bibles. That will teach people not to criticize the Bible next time around."

My point is this: The church shouldn't run and hide. We are called to engage the culture. Acts 10:38 tells us how "God anointed Jesus of Nazareth with the Holy Spirit and with power, who went about doing good." Jesus taught the gospel and He "went about doing good." That's what we are to do as well—along with sharing the gospel, we're to be "doing good."

In 1 Timothy 3:15, Paul wrote to Timothy about "how you ought to conduct yourself in the house of God, which is the church of the living God, the pillar and ground of the truth." Did you catch the definite article at the end of the verse? *The* truth. Can you imagine us standing before government officials or community leaders and saying, "Excuse me, but the Bible says the church is the pillar and the ground of the truth"? Contrast that with what the culture is saying: "Everyone has their own truth."

When it comes to engineering or technology, people can't make up their own truth. They can't arbitrarily make up the rules for how things work. Automobile and airplane manufacturers don't work that way. Imagine asking an electrical engineer, "Go ahead and wire this airplane in whatever way you feel is true to you." No one would want to ride in that airplane. There are absolutes when it comes to technology. Things have to be done correctly or they won't work right. That applies to the spiritual realm as well.

## A PRAYERFUL PULPIT

There's too much pride and arrogance in pulpits today. Too many pastors make their ministry all about themselves. But God will not share His glory with anyone. And it is a terrifying responsibility to teach from the eternal Word of God, which must be handled with great care.

The Bible has been attacked for many centuries, yet no one can find anything wrong with it. You might know people who claim, "The Bible is full of errors." But careful research and study has disproven them.

When we are prayerful, we will be the kind of church God wants us to be.

People have asked me, "At what point should I depart from my church?" My first response is, "Have you prayed for your church? Have you gone to the leadership and asked them about teaching the full counsel of God?"

If a person says yes, then I tell them, "All I can do is urge you to pray. Then see how the Lord works and do what you sense God is telling you to do." If you haven't truly committed the matter to prayer, do that before you take any other action.

Notice what Jesus said to those in the church at Philadelphia—He told the people, "I have set before you an open door, and no one can shut it; for you have a little strength" (Revelation 3:8). With Jesus as our source, "a little strength" is all we need to endure all the way to the end. He will open the doors we need to go through.

Ephesians 6 makes it clear prayer is a vital part of our spiritual armor. This gives us all the more reason to make sure our churches have prayerful pulpits. Paul wrote:

> My brethren, be strong in the Lord and in the power of His might. Put on the whole armor of God, that you may be able to stand against the wiles of the devil. For we do not wrestle against flesh and blood, but against principalities, against powers, against the rulers of the darkness of this age, against spiritual hosts of wickedness in the heavenly places. Therefore take up the whole armor of God, that you may be able to withstand in the evil day, and having done all, to stand.

Stand therefore, having girded your waist with truth, having put on the breastplate of righteousness, and having shod your feet with the preparation of the gospel of peace; above all, taking the shield of faith with which you will be able to quench all the fiery darts of the wicked one. And take the helmet of salvation, and the sword of the Spirit, which is the word of God; praying always with all prayer and supplication in the Spirit, being watchful to this end with all perseverance and supplication for all the saints.

Paul wraps up his words by urging us to be "praying always." Prayer is what keeps everything together. Through prayer, we acknowledge our complete dependence upon God. Prayer also helps us to be watchful and to persevere. In fact, nothing can happen without prayer!

## AN EXPECTANT PULPIT

Jesus has made it clear: He is coming back. We are to be alert and to watch for Him. He could come at any moment, without warning, to catch up and away His church. If we understand our Bibles correctly, there are no prophetic events that must occur before the rapture. That should make us excited and expectant!

Consider all the signs that indicate we are closer than ever to the last days: preparations to build the third temple, progress toward a global government, the technology that makes a one-world economy possible, the proliferation of evil, and more. All this tells us we're drawing nearer to the end times. And we know the rapture will take us away before the tribulation comes.

For these reasons, the pulpit should be expectant. Now, that doesn't mean we drop everything we're doing as we're waiting for the Lord to appear (John 14:1-3). Remember, we are to occupy till Jesus comes

(Luke 19:13). We're to stay busy doing His work—we're to do ministry, reach the culture for Christ, and train up the next generation of Christians. And if you're a parent or grandparent, you're to equip your children and grandchildren to be fearless and stand strong in a world that's going to challenge them.

Titus 2:13 is one of my life verses. Paul exhorts us to be "looking for the blessed hope." We're to be wide awake, watching for the "glorious appearing of our great God and Savior Jesus Christ."

In John 14:1-3, Jesus says, "Let not your heart be troubled; you believe in God, believe also in Me. In My Father's house are many mansions; if it were not so, I would have told you. I go to prepare a place for you. And if I go to prepare a place for you, I will come again and receive you to Myself, that where I am, there you may be also." That's a promise of the rapture. Jesus will come to get us and take us to His Father's house. Every pulpit should preach this hope!

## A FEARLESS PULPIT

The fear of man is killing the church. Too many Christians—including pastors—are succumbing to the expectations of the people around them.

For example, in seminary, pastors are being told they should grow big churches. But Scripture doesn't say we're to be concerned about the size of our churches. That's God's business, not ours. There are fine pastors who have congregations of 100 people, and there are some who, like C.H. Spurgeon in nineteenth-century London, have many thousands in their church. It's not the number of people that matters, but staying true to God's Word.

Some pastors are afraid to speak up about issues that might offend people. They're reluctant to proclaim the hard truths of Scripture. Such fear is carnal, and God won't bless a ministry that seeks to please people rather than Him. That's why the pulpit needs to be fearless.

Another challenge is politics in the church. Sometimes board members or specific individuals with clout will manipulate a pastor or other church members in order to get what they want. They tie the pastor's hands behind his back and make it difficult for him to do his work. As a result, the entire church is hurt.

For these reasons and more, my prayer is that pastors will be fearless, and that the sheep will encourage their pastors to be fearless. We need fearless pulpits and people.

## A FAITHFUL PULPIT

When you're finished here on earth and you stand before the Lord, here's the question that will arise: Were you faithful?

Whatever it is God has called you to do, be faithful at it. Be involved in your church. Be committed to doing Christ's work. This isn't easy—there will be times when you don't feel like going to church or fulfilling a responsibility. Sometimes ministry gets difficult or tiring.

But we're all part of the body of Christ. First Corinthians 12:12-27 makes it clear everyone has a unique place in church life. We need to lift up one another and pray for each other.

## A PROPHETIC PULPIT

In Luke 24:13, we read about two disciples who were traveling to a village called Emmaus. This took place on resurrection Sunday. They were talking with one another about Jesus' death on the cross and all that had happened since. As they conversed, Jesus joined them. "But their eyes were restrained, so that they did not know Him" (verse 16).

Jesus said to them, "What kind of conversation is this that you have with one another as you walk and are sad?" (verse 17).

Then one whose name was Cleopas answered and said to Him, "Are You the only stranger in Jerusalem, and have You not known the things which happened there in these days?"

And [Jesus] said to them, "What things?"

So they said to Him, "The things concerning Jesus of Nazareth, who was a Prophet mighty in deed and word before God and all the people, and how the chief priests and our rulers delivered Him to be condemned to death, and crucified Him. But we were hoping that it was He who was going to redeem Israel. Indeed, besides all this, today is the third day since these things happened" (verses 18-20).

These disciples were sad and disappointed. They had heard the report that some women who had arrived at the tomb early Sunday morning had found it empty. Jesus' body was no longer there. And angels at the scene had said He had risen. This confused the disciples; they weren't sure what all of this meant.

Jesus' next words to the disciples were directed not only to them, but to all people for all time. He said, "O foolish ones, and slow of heart to believe in all that the prophets have spoken! Ought not the Christ to have suffered these things and to enter into His glory?" (verses 25-26).

Then Jesus walked them through all the Old Testament prophecies that had proclaimed what He would do at His first coming. "Beginning at Moses and all the Prophets, He expounded to them in all the Scriptures the things concerning Himself" (verse 27).

How did Jesus verify He was the Son of God, the Savior who had come to redeem the lost? By pointing to what the Old Testament prophets said about Him. They had said He would suffer and die, then rise again. But the disciples hadn't grasped how God's plan would unfold. They couldn't see how the crucifixion fit into the big picture.

The New Testament church—that's us—is to do what Jesus did.

We're to carefully go through all that the Scriptures say about the coming Messiah. We're to understand the prophecies that explain what Jesus would do at His first coming. Jesus' fulfillment of these prophecies stands as confirmation that He truly is the Savior and Messiah, as prophesied in many passages.

To have a prophetic pulpit, we must proclaim God's prophetic promises, which include the message of the gospel. In doing this, we will draw people to the Savior. That's the purpose of the church: to proclaim the gospel, which is "the power of God for salvation to everyone who believes" (Romans 1:16).

When we have an authentic, engaging, prayerful, expectant, fearless, faithful, and prophetic pulpit, the church will be what Christ desires it to be, and He will bless it.

# CHAPTER 13

# THE TRIUMPHANT RETURN: WHEN JESUS COMES AS KING

## ED HINDSON

The second coming of Christ is the most anticipated event in human history. It is the ultimate fulfillment of our Lord's promise to return. It is also the culmination of all biblical prophecy. The return of Christ is the final apologetic! Once He returns, there will be no further need to debate His claims or the validity of the Christian message. The King will come in person to set the record straight.[1]

Revelation 19 is probably the most dramatic chapter in the entire Bible. It is the final capstone to the death and resurrection of Christ. In this chapter, the living Savior returns to earth to crush all satanic opposition to the truth. He establishes His kingdom on earth in fulfillment of the Old Testament prophecies of His own promise to return.

Just before the crucifixion, the disciples asked Jesus, "What will be the sign of Your coming?" (Matthew 24:3). Our Lord replied, "Immediately after the tribulation of those days...the powers of the heavens will be shaken. Then the sign of the Son of Man will appear in heaven, and then all the tribes of the earth will mourn, and they will see the Son of Man coming on the clouds of heaven with power and great glory" (verses 29-30).

As Jesus looked down the corridor of time to the end of the present age, He warned of a time of great tribulation that would come upon the whole world (verses 4-28). Our Lord went on to explain that the devastation of the great tribulation will be so extensive that unless those days were cut short, no one would survive (verse 22). Jesus further described this coming day of trouble as a time when the sun and moon will be darkened and the heavens will be shaken (verse 29). His description runs parallel to that found in Revelation 16:1-16, where the final hour of the tribulation is depicted by atmospheric darkness and ecological disaster.

The return of Christ is a twofold event. It marks both the final defeat of the antichrist and the final triumph of Christ. René Pache writes, "The main event announced by the prophets is not the judgment of the world, nor the restoration of Israel, nor even the triumph of the Church: it is the glorious advent of the Son of God."[2] Without Him, there is no hope of a better future. He is the central figure of the world to come. It is His kingdom and we are His bride. Oh, what a day that will be!

David Jeremiah observes:

> Although Christians are most familiar with the first coming of Christ, it is the second coming that gets the most ink in the Bible. References to the second coming outnumber references to the first by a factor of eight to one. Scholars count 1,845 biblical references to the second coming, including 318 in the New Testament. Christ's return is emphasized in no less than seventeen Old Testament books and seven out of every ten chapters in the New Testament. The Lord Himself referred to His return twenty-one times.

The second coming is second only to faith as the most dominant subject in the New Testament.[3]

## THE PROMISE OF HIS RETURN

Jesus promised His disciples in the upper room that He was going to heaven to prepare a place for them. Then He said, "If I go and prepare a place for you, I will come again and receive you to Myself; that where I am, there you may be also" (John 14:3). Even though the early disciples eventually died, the Bible promised, "Behold, I tell you a mystery: We shall not all sleep [die], but we shall all be changed [resurrected or raptured]—in a moment, in the twinkling of an eye, at the last trumpet. For the trumpet will sound, and the dead will be raised incorruptible, and we shall be changed" (1 Corinthians 15:51-52).

The apostle Paul reiterates this same hope in 1 Thessalonians 4:14, 16-17 when he comments about those believers who have already died and gone to heaven. He says, "If we believe that Jesus died and rose again, even so God will bring with Him [from heaven] those who have fallen asleep [died] in Jesus…For the Lord Himself will descend from heaven with a shout, with the voice of the archangel and with the trumpet of God; and the dead in Christ will rise first. Then we who are alive and remain will be caught up together with them in the clouds to meet the Lord in the air" (NASB 1995).

The promise to return for the church (believers of the church age) is the promise of the rapture. When Revelation 19 opens, the church is already in heaven with Christ at the marriage supper. The rapture has already occurred. Jesus is depicted as the groom and the church as the bride. The marriage supper celebrates their union after the rapture and before their return to earth.

One of the greatest interpretive problems for nonrapturists is to explain how the church got to heaven *prior* to the second coming.

Surely they were not all martyred, or else Paul's comments about "we who are alive and remain" (1 Thessalonians 4:15, 17) would be meaningless. The rapture must be presumed to have occurred before the events in Revelation 19—amillennialists and post-millennialists notwithstanding.[4]

The position of the church (bride of the Lamb) in Revelation 19:6-10 in *heaven* is crucial to the interpretation of the entire apocalypse. New Testament scholar Robert Gromacki points out, "The Church is not mentioned during the seal, trumpet and bowl judgments because the Church is not here during the outpouring of these judgments."[5] He points out that the term for *church* (Greek, *ekklesia*) appears frequently in chapters 1–3 of Revelation. In fact, it is used 19 times in those chapters. But the word *church* does not appear again until 22:16. In the meantime, the church is referred to in 19:7-10 as the bride of the Lamb.

The concept of the church as the bride or wife of Christ is clearly stated in Ephesians 5:22-23, where husbands are admonished to love their wives as Christ loved the church and gave Himself for her that He might present her in heaven as a glorious bride. There can be no doubt, therefore, that John intends for us to see the Lamb's "wife" as the church—the bride of Christ.

## THE NATURE OF CHRIST'S RETURN

Jesus promised not only to return for His church, but He also promised to return to judge the world and to establish His kingdom on earth. James refers to believers as "heirs of the kingdom which He promised to those who love Him" (James 2:5). Jesus Himself told His disciples that He would not drink the fruit of the vine after the Last Supper until He drank it with them in His Father's kingdom (Matthew 26:29). After the resurrection, they asked Him, "Lord, will You at this time restore the kingdom to Israel?" (Acts 1:6). He replied that the time was in the Father's hands. All these references imply a future kingdom when Christ returns.

The details of Christ's return include the following:

### He Will Return Personally

Paul said, "The Lord Himself will descend from heaven with a shout" (1 Thessalonians 4:16). Jesus promised He would return in person (Matthew 24:30).

### He Will Appear as the Son of Man

Since Pentecost, Christ has ministered through the Holy Spirit (John 14:16-23; 16:5-15). But when He returns, He will appear as the Son of Man in His glorified human form (Matthew 24:30; 26:64; Daniel 7:13-14).

### He Will Return Literally and Visibly

In Acts 1:11, the angels promised, "This Jesus, who has been taken up from you into heaven, will come in just the same way as you have watched Him go into heaven" (NASB 1995). Revelation 1:7 tells us, "Every eye will see Him, even those who pierced Him; and all the tribes of the earth will mourn over Him" (NASB 1995).

### He Will Come Suddenly and Dramatically

Paul warned, "The day of the Lord so comes as a thief in the night" (1 Thessalonians 5:2). Jesus said, "As the lightning comes from the east and flashes to the west, so also will the coming of the Son of Man be" (Matthew 24:27).

### He Will Come on the Clouds of Heaven

Jesus said, "They will see the Son of Man coming on the clouds of heaven" (Matthew 24:30 [See Daniel 7:13; Luke 21:27]). Revelation 1:7 says, "Behold, He is coming with clouds."

### He Will Come in a Display of Glory

Matthew 16:27 promises, "The Son of Man will come in the glory of His Father." Matthew 24:30 adds, "They will see the Son of Man coming…with power and great glory."

### He Will Come with All His Angels

Jesus promised, "He will send His angels with a great sound of a trumpet" (Matthew 24:31). Jesus said in one of His parables, "The reapers are the angels…so it will be at the end of this age" (Matthew 13:39-40).

### He Will Come with His Bride, the Church

That, of course, is the whole point of Revelation 19. Colossians 3:4 adds, "When Christ…appears, then you also will appear with Him in glory." Zechariah 14:5 adds, "Then the LORD, my God, will come, and all the holy ones with Him!" (NASB 1995).

### He Will Return to the Mount of Olives

"In that day His feet will stand on the Mount of Olives" (Zechariah 14:4). Where the glory of God ascended into heaven, it will return (cf. Ezekiel 11:23). Where Jesus ascended into heaven, He will return (cf. Acts 1:3-12).

### He Will Return in Triumph and Victory

Zechariah 14:9 promises, "The LORD shall be King over all the earth." Revelation 19:16 depicts Him as "KING OF KINGS AND LORD OF LORDS." He will triumph over the antichrist, the false prophet, and Satan himself (Revelation 19:19-21).

## HALLELUJAH, WHAT A SAVIOR!

Revelation 19 opens with a heavenly chorus, a "great multitude" singing the praises of God (verse 1). G.R. Beasley-Murray calls it a "*Te Deum* [hymn of praise to God] on the righteous judgments of God."[6]

The heavenly choir rejoices with praise because justice has finally been served: "True and righteous are His judgments," they sing, "because He has judged the great harlot" (verse 2). The praise chorus then breaks into a fourfold alleluia in verses 1-6:

1. "Alleluia! Salvation and glory and honor and power belong to the Lord our God!" (verse 1).

2. "Alleluia! Her smoke rises up forever and ever!" (verse 3).

3. They "worshiped God who sat on the throne, saying, 'Amen! Alleluia!'" (verse 4).

4. "Alleluia! For the Lord God Omnipotent reigns!" (verse 6).

This is the only place in the New Testament where *alleluia* (or *hallelujah*) occurs. It is a Hebrew word ("Praise Yah [Jehovah]"). It was transliterated from the Hebrew into Greek and passed on into English. The same thing occurred with *amen, hosanna,* and *maranatha.* The use of the four alleluias emphasizes the magnitude of this praise and worship.

Beasley-Murray observes that these alleluias are reminiscent of the Hallel Psalms (113–118), which were sung at the Jewish Passover meal.[7] The first two (113–114) were sung before the meal and the last four after the meal. Just as Israel sang God's praises for His deliverance in the Passover, so the church in heaven will sing God's praise for His deliverance from the antichrist. The triumphal praise is very similar to that heard earlier in Revelation 11:15-19. But the triumph that is heralded is more than that over the downfall of Babylon. It is the marriage of the Lamb that takes center stage in this cantata of praise.

## MARRIAGE OF THE LAMB

The sense of movement always prevalent in the apocalypse now reaches a climax. "The marriage of the Lamb has come" (Revelation 19:7).

It is as though we have finally arrived at what we have been waiting for all along. The wedding is finally here. It is obvious that John the revelator views this as a future (not past) event. The final culmination of the spiritual union between the Lamb and His bride has finally arrived.

Beasley-Murray expresses it like this: "The perfection in glory of the *Bride* belongs to the eschatological future! Therefore, the *now* and the *not yet* of the New Testament doctrine of salvation in the kingdom of God is perfectly exemplified. The Church is the Bride of Christ now, but her marriage lies in the future."[8]

This is why we cannot say that the consummation of the marriage has already taken place. The apostle Paul says, "I have betrothed you to one husband, that I may present you as a chaste virgin to Christ" (2 Corinthians 11:2). He also adds that Christ "loved the church and gave Himself for her...that He might present her to Himself a glorious church, not having spot or wrinkle or any such thing, but that she should be holy and without blemish" (Ephesians 5:25-27).

Bruce Metzger comments, "The concept of the relationship between God and his people as a marriage goes back into the Old Testament. Again and again the prophets spoke of Israel as the chosen Bride of God (Is. 54:1-8; Ezek. 16:7,8; Hos. 2:19). In the New Testament the Church is represented as the Bride of Christ...In the words of a familiar hymn: 'With his own blood he bought her, and for her life he died.'"[9]

## THE TRIUMPHAL RETURN

The singular vignette of Christ's return in Revelation 19:11-16 is the most dramatic passage in the entire Bible. In these six verses, we are swept up into the triumphal entourage of redeemed saints as they ride in the heavenly procession with the King of kings and Lord of lords. In this one passage alone, all the hopes and dreams of every believer are finally and fully realized. This is not the Palm

Sunday procession with the humble Messiah on the donkey colt. This is the ultimate in eschatological drama. The rejected Savior returns in triumph as the rightful King of all the world—*and we are with Him!*

Metzger notes, "From here on the tempo of the action increases. The ultimate outcome cannot be in doubt, but there are some surprises ahead, with the suspense of the drama sustained to the conclusion. From verse 11 to the first verse of chapter 21, we have in rapid succession seven visions preparatory to the end. Each of these begins with the word, 'I saw.'"[10]

The description of the triumphant Savior is that of a king leading an army to victory. The passage itself describes the final phase of the seventh bowl judgment begun in 16:17-21, moving through the details of 17:1–18:24 and on to chapter 19. Robert Thomas observes: "The final song of 19:1-8 celebrates the marriage of the warrior-Messiah...This agrees closely with traditional Jewish eschatology. The O.T. prophets foresaw the Lord coming in the Last Days as a man of war to dash his enemies in pieces and establish a kingdom over the nations (e.g., Isaiah 13:4; 31:4; 42:13; Ezek. 38–39; Joel 3; Zech. 14:3)."[11]

As the scene unfolds, heaven opens to reveal the Christ and to release the army of the redeemed. The description of their being clothed in bright, clean linen (Revelation 19:14) emphasizes the garments of the bride already mentioned earlier (verse 8). In this vignette, the bride appears as the army of the Messiah. But unlike contemporary apocalyptic dramas of that time (e.g., the War Scroll of the Qumran sect), the victory is won without any military help from the faithful. This army has no weapons, no swords, no shields, and no armor. They are merely clad in the righteousness of the saints. They have not come to fight but to watch. They have not come to assist but to celebrate. The Messiah-King will do the fighting. He will win the battle by the power of His spoken word.

## THE TWELVEFOLD
## DESCRIPTION OF THE KING

The twelvefold description of the coming King (Revelation 19:11-16) combines elements of symbolism from various biblical passages and from the other pictures of the risen Christ in the book of Revelation. Notice the details of His appearance:

### 1. His Conquest: He Rides the White Horse (Revelation 19:11)

Revelation 19:11 describes Jesus arriving on a white horse. A white horse symbolized victory. Unlike the usurper who rides the white horse in Revelation 6:2, this rider is called "Faithful and True" (verse 11). Jesus will return to win in battle over Satan and His enemies in fulfillment of numerous prophecies regarding His second coming.

### 2. His Character: He Is Called Faithful and True (Revelation 3:14)

The declaration of Jesus as the faithful and true one in Revelation 19 connects with the message to the church at Laodicea in Revelation 3:14: "These things says the Amen, the Faithful and True Witness, the Beginning of the creation of God." The context of Revelation 3 and the messages to the seven churches clearly indicate Jesus is speaking. It is the magnitude of His character that will ultimately triumph over evil.

### 3. His Commission: He Judges and Makes War
### (2 Thessalonians 1:7-8)

In 2 Thessalonians 1:7-8, Paul speaks about Jesus, saying He will "give you who are troubled rest with us when the Lord Jesus is revealed from heaven with His mighty angels, in flaming fire taking vengeance on those who do not know God, and on those who do not obey the gospel of our Lord Jesus Christ." Paul clearly and accurately describes the second coming. Jesus will return from heaven with His angels, judging unbelievers in war against those who oppose Him.

### 4. His Clarity: His Eyes Are Like a Flame of Fire (Revelation 1:14)

Revelation 1:14 describes Jesus in His glorified state: "His head and hair were white like wool, as white as snow, and His eyes like a flame of fire." These words echo Revelation 19:12, where Jesus returns with similar eyes: "His eyes were like a flame of fire." This indicates the penetration of His omniscient gaze into the souls of men.

### 5. His Coronation: He Wears Many Crowns (Revelation 4:10)

Likewise, Revelation 4:10 also describes the glorified Jesus as receiving many crowns: "The twenty-four elders fall down before Him who sits on the throne and worship Him who lives forever and ever, and cast their crowns before the throne." This closely connects with Revelation 19:12, where we read, "On His head were many crowns" (Greek, *diadems*). He returns wearing the multiple crowns of His Kingship.

### 6. His Code: His Secret Name (Judges 13:18; Isaiah 9:6)

Revelation 19:12 indicates that He is identified with the secret, unspoken name of God. The I AM of the Old Testament (YHVH) was held in such high regard that His name was unspoken (Exodus 3:13-15). The revelation of this name makes public the name of the Messiah. Isaiah spoke of the coming Jewish Messiah in 9:6, declaring: "And His name will be called Wonderful, Counselor, Mighty God, Everlasting Father, Prince of Peace." The second coming of Jesus will reveal the child born in the manger is the one who rules the world, equal with God the Father.

### 7. His Clothing: Robe Dipped in Blood (Isaiah 63:1-6)

Revelation 19:13 includes the note, "He was clothed with a robe dipped in blood," referring to the blood of His enemies. These words closely reflect the prophecy of Isaiah 63:1-6. For example, verses 2-3 tell us:

Why is Your apparel red,
and Your garments like one who treads in the winepress?
"I have trodden the winepress alone,
and from the peoples no one was with Me.
For I have trodden them in My anger,
and trampled them in My fury;
their blood is sprinkled upon My garments,
and I have stained all My robes."

This graphically shows that the second coming will include much violence. During Christ's first coming, He shed His own blood. At the second coming, He will shed the blood of His enemies, bringing judgment upon those who have opposed Him.

### 8. His Confirmation: Called the Word of God (John 1:1)

Revelation 19:13 identifies the being at the second coming as "The Word of God." This phrase closely connects with the apostle John's words at the beginning of his Gospel, where we read, "In the beginning was the Word, and the Word was with God, and the Word was God." Further, the mention of Jesus as the "Word of God" also identifies Him as more than just the Messiah, but as equal with God the Father. Jesus was "in the beginning with God" (John 1:2) and is co-eternal and co-existent with the Father and the Holy Spirit. Verse 3 adds, "All things were made through Him, and without Him nothing was made that was made." The author of creation will return at the second coming to redeem His world and reign from His throne.

### 9. His Communication: Sword Is in His Mouth (Revelation 19:15, 21)

He who created the world by His spoken word will conquer the world by that word. Revelation 19:15 notes a sharp sword from the mouth of Jesus that will strike the nations. Similarly, in Revelation 2:16,

Jesus says He "will fight against them with the sword of My mouth." This is clearly the Lord, the one spoken of as the Messiah in Isaiah 49:2:

> He has made My mouth like a sharp sword;
> in the shadow of His hand He has hidden Me,
> and made Me a polished shaft;
> in His quiver He has hidden Me.

The Lord will use the sword of His mouth to conquer His enemies and establish His kingdom at this final battle. He speaks, and the battle is over! The greatest conflagration in human history will come to an end with Christ and His church at last victorious.

### 10. His Command: Rules with a Rod of Iron (Psalm 2:9)

In Revelation 19:15, Christ states He will "rule them with a rod of iron." This is one of three times the phrase "rod of iron" is used in Revelation. In 2:27, Jesus predicts, "He shall rule them with a rod of iron." In 12:5, the male Child (Jesus) "was to rule all nations with a rod of iron." These prophecies connect with the words of the psalmist in Psalm 2:9:

> You shall break them with a rod of iron;
> You shall dash them to pieces like a potter's vessel.

This is clearly the Messiah, the one who says in 2:7,

> I will declare the decree:
> the LORD has said to Me,
> "You are My Son,
> Today I have begotten You."

Jesus will fulfill this promise when He returns, wielding ultimate authority during His millennial kingdom here on earth, where we will reign with Him.

### 11. His Conquest: Treads the Winepress of the Wrath of God (Revelation 14:14-20)

We've already mentioned the connection of the winepress with Isaiah 63. However, this fulfillment at the second coming also connects with John's earlier words in Revelation 14. The graphic description is given of God's judgment in verse 20: "The winepress was trampled outside the city, and blood came out of the winepress, up to the horses' bridles, for one thousand six hundred furlongs."

The height of a horse's bridle is usually estimated at about four-and-a-half feet. The distance of the bloody image in this prediction of 1,600 furlongs (or literally 1,600 stadia) is approximately 180 miles. This would indicate an area larger than Armageddon, extending beyond to neighboring locations past the Jezreel Valley. Regardless of the exact details, the gruesome picture depicted here indicates the most destructive judgment possible, in which the enemies of God will be completely annihilated.

### 12. His Celebration: King of Kings and Lord of Lords (Revelation 17:14)

The name King of kings and Lord of lords, found in Revelation 19:16, is used in Scripture to describe the greatest of leaders (Ezra 7:12; Ezekiel 26:7; Daniel 2:37, 47). In the New Testament, it is used in 1 Timothy 6:15 about Jesus. Revelation 17:14 is the one other mention of this name in John's prophecy, where the name is also associated with the Lamb. Similarly, those with Him are described as "called, chosen, and faithful." As Warren Wiersbe notes:

> This description of Christ is thrilling! He is no longer on a humble donkey, but on a fiery white charger. His eyes are not filled with tears as when He beheld Jerusalem; nor is He wearing a mocking crown of thorns. Instead of being stripped by His enemies, He wears a garment dipped in

blood, signifying judgment and victory. When on earth, He was abandoned by His followers; but here the armies of heaven follow Him in conquest. His mouth does not speak "words of grace" (Luke 4:22), but rather the Word of victory and justice.[12]

The Savior will return from heaven with His bride at His side. The church militant is now the church triumphant. Her days of conflict, rejection, and persecution are over. She returns victorious with her Warrior-King-Husband. The German pietist A.W. Boehm put it best when he wrote:

> There will be a time when the Church of Christ will come up from the wilderness of her crosses and afflictions, leaning upon her Beloved, and in his power bidding defiance to all her enemies. Then shall the Church…appear Terrible as an Army with banners, but terrible to those only that despised her while she was in her minority and would not have her Beloved to reign over them.[13]

Every true believer who reads the prediction of Christ's triumph in Revelation 19:11-16 is overwhelmed by its significance. We are also overcome by its personal implications, for each of us will be in that heavenly army that returns with Him from glory. In fact, you might want to take a pen and circle the word "armies" in 19:14 and write your name in the margin of your Bible next to it, for *every believer* will be there when He returns.

The destiny of the true believer is now fully clarified. Our future hope includes rapture, return, and reign. No matter what one's eschatological viewpoint, the church must be raptured to heaven prior to the marriage supper and prior to her return from heaven with Christ. In the rapture, we will go up to heaven. In the return, we will come back to earth. In the millennium, we will reign with Christ on the earth for 1,000 years (Revelation 20:4-6).

## HOW WILL JESUS RETURN?

We've looked at the chronology of Jesus' return at His second coming, as well as the twelvefold description of the King. In addition, Scripture also reveals seven aspects of how Jesus will return that encourage us regarding our amazing future with Him.

### Personally

Of utmost importance is the promise that Christ will return personally. He will not send others on His behalf, but will be intimately involved with the culmination of His prophetic plans. In Acts 1:10-11, the disciples looked up at the sky where Jesus had ascended to the Father in heaven. Two angels appeared, saying, "Men of Galilee, why do you stand gazing up into heaven? This same Jesus, who was taken up from you into heaven, will so come in like manner as you saw Him go into heaven." Just as Jesus personally left this world, He will personally return to it.

Revelation 22:20 also assures us of His personal involvement: "He who testifies to these things says, 'Surely I am coming quickly.'" Jesus does not say He will send for us; He will come for us. The one who made us and sustains us will return for us at the rapture and return with us at the second coming to establish a throne that will ultimately last for all eternity.

### Literally

I am amazed at those who argue Jesus will fulfill His prophecies only symbolically. While some aspects of Bible prophecy are symbolic, His second coming will result in the literal fulfillment of multiple predictions. Revelation 19 offers numerous details of Jesus literally coming, unleashing judgment, and defeating His enemies. He will not outsource His victory but will appear in person for this final battle at the end of the tribulation period, and we will be with Him (Revelation 19:14). Jesus will return with His bride, not to spare the church, but to spare the human race. He Himself predicted, "Unless those days were shortened, no flesh would be saved" (Matthew 24:22).

### Visibly

In many films about the rapture, those who go to be with the Lord simply disappear. In some cases, their clothing is left behind to show the person is no longer on earth. While some details of how we will ascend at the rapture are unclear, we do know the event will occur quickly, leaving many people wondering what took place.

However, the second coming will present a strong contrast. Jesus will return visibly to earth to judge His enemies. Matthew 24:23-27 describes a clear arrival of the Lord. Verse 27 says, "As the lightning comes from the east and flashes to the west, so also will the coming of the Son of Man be." Everyone will know when the Lord arrives at the second coming. As eventful as Christ's arrival was in Jerusalem on Palm Sunday, it will not compare with the ultimate triumph with which He will arrive at the end of the tribulation.

### Suddenly

Similar to the rapture, the second coming will take place suddenly. Revelation 3:3 states, "I will come upon you as a thief, and you will not know what hour I will come upon you." In Matthew 24:44, Jesus also warned His disciples in the parable of the watchful homeowner, "Therefore you also be ready, for the Son of Man is coming at an hour you do not expect." This is true not only of the rapture but of the return as well in regard to the unsaved. In both instances, unbelievers will remain unexpectant of the Lord's coming.

### Dramatically

In addition to coming suddenly, Christ will return at His second coming dramatically. Matthew 24:29 teaches, "Immediately after the tribulation of those days the sun will be darkened, and the moon will not give its light; the stars will fall from heaven, and the powers of the heavens will be shaken." As mentioned earlier, these signs will take place as part of the Lord's return while the world is under severe judgment. The light of the sun and moon will not be visible, while the stars will appear as though falling. These dramatic signs will signal the time of the Lord's return.

### Gloriously

The second coming will include Jesus returning gloriously. Matthew 24:30 describes Jesus as arriving with great power and glory. Second Thessalonians 1:7 predicts Jesus will return with His mighty angels. This will serve as a royal, splendid appearance that Paul calls a "glorious appearing." According to Titus 2:11-13:

> The grace of God that brings salvation has appeared to all men, teaching us that, denying ungodliness and worldly lusts, we should live soberly, righteously, and godly in the present age, looking for the blessed hope and glorious appearing of our great God and Savior Jesus Christ.

### Triumphantly

Ultimately, Jesus will return triumphantly. Revelation 19:19-21 speaks of the destruction of Christ's enemies and the victory He will win upon His appearing. Jesus triumphed over sin and death through His resurrection (Colossians 2:15). At His return, He will triumph again as He conquers His enemies and begins His millennial reign.

Christ's dramatic and triumphant return will effectively set the stage for His millennial reign and the eternal state to follow. The marriage of the Lamb began the opening ceremonies in heaven. Now the King and His bride will rule for 1,000 years on the earth as the devastated planet again blossoms like a rose.

And you and I will be there!

# ABOUT THE CONTRIBUTORS

**Jan Markell** is the founder and president of Olive Tree Ministries. Her radio outreach, *Understanding the Times*, is now heard on 1,000 radio stations across North America and around the world electronically. She continues to host bimonthly prophecy events that are held by Olive Tree Ministries and Mark Henry Ministries, and she is the author of *Understanding the Times*.

**Amir Tsarfati** is a native Israeli and the founder and president of Behold Israel—a nonprofit ministry that provides Bible teaching through tours, conferences, and social media. It also provides unique access to news and information about Israel from a biblical and prophetic standpoint. He is the author of several books, including *Discovering Daniel* and *Revealing Revelation*.

**Jeff Kinley** (ThM, Dallas Theological Seminary) has authored more than 40 books, and his podcasts, *The Prophecy Pros Podcast* and *Vintage Truth*, are heard in more than 130 countries. His weekly His-Channel TV shows, *Jeff Kinley Live* and *The King Is Coming*, are devoted to Bible prophecy.

**Michele Bachmann** (JD, LLM) is the Dean of the Robertson School of Government at Regent University in Virginia. She is a former US Congresswoman (R Minn) in the House of Representatives (2007–2015) and a highly respected leader who is deeply committed to conservative values in government.

**Mark Hitchcock** (ThM, PhD, Dallas Theological Seminary) has authored more than 30 books related to Bible prophecy and is the

Research Professor of Bible Exposition at Dallas Theological Seminary. He is the senior pastor of Faith Bible Church in Edmond, Oklahoma.

**Jack Hibbs** is the senior and founding pastor of Calvary Chapel Chino Hills in Southern California, and is the author of *Living in the Daze of Deception*. He is also the host of the nationally syndicated TV and radio program *Real Life*, and his daily media programs reach millions worldwide.

**Erwin W. Lutzer** is pastor emeritus of The Moody Church, where he served as the senior pastor for 36 years. He is an award-winning author of many books, including *We Will Not Be Silenced*, and the featured speaker on two radio programs heard on more than 750 outlets worldwide.

**Anne Morrow Graham Lotz** is an American evangelist, the second daughter of evangelist Billy Graham and his wife Ruth Graham. She founded AnGeL Ministries, is the author of 11 books, is the teacher on the *Living in the Light* radio program, and is a popular speaker all over the globe.

**Barry Stagner** is the founding and senior pastor of Calvary Chapel OC in Southern California. A trusted teacher on Bible prophecy, he is the host of *The Line Up*, a weekly broadcast heard worldwide, and the author of *Times of the Signs*.

**Ed Hindson** was formerly Dean Emeritus of the School of Divinity and Distinguished Professor of Religion at Liberty University in Virginia and the speaker on *The King Is Coming* telecast. He both authored and served as the general editor of 40-plus books, including *Can We Still Believe in the Rapture?* and *Future Glory*.

# NOTES

## CHAPTER 1—HIDDEN IN PLAIN VIEW:
## THE NEW WORLD ORDER IN BIBLE PROPHECY

1. Julian Hattem, "Trump warns against 'false song of globalism,' " *The Hill*, April 27, 2016, https://thehill.com/policy/national-security/277879-trump-warns-against-false-song-of-globalism/.

2. *Clinton Global Initiative* home page, https://www.clintonfoundation.org/programs/leadership-public-service/clinton-global-initiative/.

3. Peter Grose, *Continuing the Inquiry: The Council on Foreign Relations from 1921 to 1996* (New York: Council on Foreign Relations Press, 2006), 48.

4. Carroll Quigley, *Tragedy and Hope: A History of the World in Our Time* (New York: MacMillan, 1966), 950-951.

5. "About us," *The Club of Rome*, https://www.clubofrome.org/about-us/.

6. Home page, *The Club of Rome*, https://www.clubofrome.org/.

7. Henry Kissinger at the World Affairs Council press conference, Regent Beverly Wilshire Hotel, April 19, 1994.

8. David Rockefeller, as cited in "New World Order Quotes," *No World System*, https://infolution.wordpress.com/what-is-the-new-world-order/.

9. David Rockefeller, *Memoirs* (New York: Random House, 2003), 405.

10. George Bush, "Address Before a Joint Session of the Congress on the State of the Union," *The American Presidency Project*, January 29, 1991, https://www.presidency.ucsb.edu/documents/address-before-joint-session-the-congress-the-state-the-union-1.

11. Pope Francis, "Encyclical Letter *Fratelli Tutti* of the Holy Father Francis on Fraternity and Social Friendship," *The Holy See*, October 3, 2020, https://www.vatican.va/content/francesco/en/encyclicals/documents/papa-francesco_20201003_enciclica-fratelli-tutti.html.

12. Pope John Paul II, "Address of the Holy Father John Paul II to H.E. Mr. Oded Ben-Hur New Ambassador of Israel to the Holy See," *The Holy See*, June 2, 2003, https://www.vatican.va/content/john-paul-ii/en/speeches/2003/june/documents/hf_jp-ii_spe_20030602_ambassador-israel.html.

13. Alex Howe, "The Truth About George Soros' Radical Vision to Remake the Entire World," *Business Insider*, October 4, 2011, https://www.businessinsider.com/george-soros-new-world-order-2011-9.

14. George Soros, *Open Society* (New York: Public Affairs, 2000), xvi.

15. "Who Is Helping Biden Facilitate America's Border Crisis?," *The Heritage Foundation*, December 19, 2022, https://www.heritage.org/homeland-security/heritage-explains/who-helping-biden-facilitate-americas-border-crisis.

16. Chris Bennett, "Doomsday Addiction: Celebrating 50 Years of Failed Climate Predictions," *AG Web*, May 2, 2023, https://www.agweb.com/opinion/doomsday-addiction-celebrating-50-years-failed-climate-predictions.

17. Ian Johnson, "Seven in 10 Brits support 'world government' to protect humanity from global catastrophes," *Independent*, June 8, 2017, https://www.independent.co.uk/climate-change/news/climate-change-global-warming-nuclear-war-asteroid-pandemic-volcano-global-catastrophe-a7752171.html.

18. Penny Starr, "UN: Humans Could Cause Extinction of 1 Million Species, Globalism Will Fix," *Breitbart*, May 6, 2019, https://www.breitbart.com/politics/2019/05/06/un-humans-could-cause-extinction-of-1-million-species-globalism-will-fix/.

19. Larry Bell, "In Their Own Words: Climate Alarmists Debunk Their 'Science,'" *Forbes*, February 5, 2013, https://www.forbes.com/sites/larrybell/2013/02/05/in-their-own-words-climate-alarmists-debunk-their-science/?sh=7c15a01368a3.

20. "IIX Foundation partners with Green Cross to bring women to the forefront of climate action," *IIX*, https://iixglobal.com/iix-foundation-partners-green-cross-for-she-is-more/.

## CHAPTER 3—PERILOUS TIMES: WHEN AMERICA ABANDONS THE ROLE OF GLOBAL LEADERSHIP

1. "Timeline of Christian Missions," *Wikipedia*, https://en.wikipedia.org/wiki/Timeline_of_Christian_missions.

2. William Bradford, *Of Plymouth Plantation* (Enhanced Media, 2017), 46, https://www.google.com/books/edition/Of_Plymouth_Plantation/00r6DQAAQBAJ?hl=en&gbpv=1&dq=%22When+they+were+ready+to+depart,+they+had+a+day+of+solemn+humiliation%22&pg=PA46&printsec=frontcover.

3. Bradford, *Of Plymouth Plantation*, 46.

4. Bradford, *Of Plymouth Plantation*, 46.

5. Bradford, *Of Plymouth Plantation*, 46-47.

6. Dan Graves, "Yale Founded to Fight Liberalism," *Christianity.com*, April 28, 2010, https://www.christianity.com/church/church-history/timeline/1701-1800/yale-founded-to-fight-liberalism-11630185.html.

7. Thomas Jefferson Wertenbaker, *Princeton, 1746-1896* (Princeton, NJ: Princeton University Press, 1946), 19.

8. William Blackstone, *Commentaries* 39 and 40.

9. Mandeep S. Tiwana, "Agenda 2030: Why civic participation is key to meeting UN sustainability targets," *World Economic Forum*, April 24, 2023, https://www.weforum.org/agenda/2023/04/agenda-2030-civic-participation-sustainable-development-goals/.

10. Slobhán O'Grady, "Khamenei to Israel: You Will Not Exist in 25 Years," *Foreign Policy*, September 9, 2015, https://foreignpolicy.com/2015/09/09/khamenei-to-israel-you-will-not-exist-in-25-years/.

11. Lizzy Cohn, "Showdown in the Spratleys: How Economics Drives China's Claims in the South China Sea," *Michigan Journal of Economics*, January 31, 2024, https://sites.lsa.umich.edu/mje/2024/01/31/showdown-in-the-spratleys-how-economics-drives-chinas-claims-in-the-south-china-sea/.

12. Benjamin Jensen, "How the Chinese Communist Party Uses Cyber Espionage to Undermine the American Economy," *Center for Strategic & International Studies*, October 19, 2023, https://www.csis.org/analysis/how-chinese-communist-party-uses-cyber-espionage-undermine-american-economy.

## CHAPTER 4—OUR BLESSED HOPE: THE RAPTURE OF THE CHURCH

1. "How Fast Is the Average Blink?," *Soma Technology*, August 6, 2020, https://www.somatechnology.com/blog/thursday-thoughts/fast-average-blink/.

2. Ed Hindson and Mark Hitchcock, *Can We Still Believe in the Rapture?* (Eugene, OR: Harvest House, 2018).

3. John F. Walvoord, *The Rapture Question* (Grand Rapids, MI: Zondervan, 1957), 191-199.

4. "Rock of Ages," Augustus Toplady, 1776.

## CHAPTER 6—WHY WE CAN STILL BELIEVE IN A RAPTURE

1. Emil Brunner, *Eternal Hope*, trans. Harold Knight (Philadelphia, PA: The Westminster Press, 1954), 138-139.

2. Pew Research Center Report, "Global Survey of Evangelical Protestant Leaders—Evangelical Beliefs and Practices," *Pew Research Center*, June 22, 2011, https://www.pewresearch.org/religion/2011/06/22/global-survey-beliefs/.

## CHAPTER 7—ONE MINUTE AFTER YOU DIE

1. Bishop James A. Pike, *The Other Side* (New York: Dell, 1969).

2. Rob Bell, *Love Wins* (New York: Harper One, 2012).

3. "My Hope Is Built on Nothing Less," Edward Mote, 1834.

## CHAPTER 8—A WARNING TO AMERICA FROM THE BOOK OF JOEL

1. "Inside the Aftermath of South Carolina's Devastating Floods," *ABC News*, October 6, 2015, https://abcnews.go.com/US/inside-aftermath-south-carolinas-devastating-flooding/story?id=34279677#:~:text=From%20Charleston%20to%20Columbia%2C%20the,a%20storm%20of%20historic%20proportions.%22.

2. "Tornado Outbreak August 24, 2016," *National Weather Service*, https://www.weather.gov/iwx/20160824_TornadoOutbreak.

3. Elizabeth Rivelli, "Drunk driving statistics," *Bankrate*, https://www.bankrate.com/insurance/car/drunk-driving/.

4. "Alcoholism Statistics You Need to Know," *Talbott Recovery*, https://talbottcampus.com/alcoholism-statistics/.

5. "Alcohol-Related Crimes," *Alcohol Rehab Guide*, updated November 14, 2023, https://www.alcoholrehabguide.org/alcohol/crimes.

6. "Marijuana and Teens," *American Academy of Child & Adolescent Psychiatry*, updated September 2023, https://www.aacap.org/AACAP/Families_and_Youth/Facts_for_Families/FFF-Guide/Marijuana-and-Teens-106.aspx.

7. "Cannabis (Marijuana) DrugFacts," *National Institute on Drug Abuse*, December 2019, https://nida.nih.gov/publications/drugfacts/cannabis-marijuana.

8. Daniel F. McCaffrey, Rosalie Liccardo Pacula, Bing Han, and Phyllis Ellickson, "Marijuana Use and High School Dropout: The Influence of Unobservables," *National Library of Medicine*, https://www.ncbi.nlm.nih.gov/pmc/articles/PMC2910149/#:~:text=In%20their%20models%20they%20find,of%20high%20school%20than%20nonusers.

9. Kathleen E. Feeney and Kyle M. Kampman, "Adverse effects of marijuana use," *National Library of Medicine*, https://www.ncbi.nlm.nih.gov/pmc/articles/PMC5102212/#:~:text=Roughly%20two%2Dthirds%20of%20high,Miech%20et%20al.%202015).&text=found%20that%20about%2012%20percent,rates%20of%20use%20among%20youth.

10. "Drug Overdose Death Rates," *National Institute on Drug Abuse*, https://nida.nih.gov/research-topics/trends-statistics/overdose-death-rates.

11. "Suicide," *National Institute of Mental Health*, https://www.nimh.nih.gov/health/statistics/suicide.

12. "Difference between the inflation rate and growth of wages in the United States from March 2020 to March 2024," *statista*, April 19, 2024, https://www.statista.com/statistics/1351276/wage-growth-vs-inflation-us/.

13. Elizabeth Schulze, "American's credit card debt hits record $1.13 trillion," *ABC News*, February 6, 2024, https://abcnews.go.com/US/americans-credit-card-debt-hits-record-113-trillion/story?id=106990807.

14. "What Is the National Debt Today?," *Peter G. Peterson Foundation*, accessed April 20, 2024, https://www.pgpf.org/national-debt-clock.

15. Romina Boccia and Dominik Lett, "The CBO Budget and Economic Outlook: Debt Projected to Grow to Record Highs," *Cato Institute*, February 8, 2024, https://www.cato.org/blog/cbo-budget-economic-outlook-debt-projected-grow-record-highs.

16. Joe Pinsker, "The Hidden Economics of Porn," *The Atlantic*, April 4, 2016, https://www.the-atlantic.com/business/archive/2016/04/pornography-industry-economics-tarrant/476580/.

17. Kanishka Singh, "Over 70% of Jewish college students exposed to antisemitism this school year, survey finds," *Reuters*, November 29, 2023, https://www.reuters.com/world/us/over-70-us-jewish-college-students-exposed-antisemitism-this-school-year-survey-2023-11-29/.

18. "11 Facts About 9/11," *dosomething.org*, https://www.dosomething.org/us/facts/11-facts-about-911.

## CHAPTER 9—APOSTASY: THE SABOTAGE
## OF CHRISTIANITY FROM WITHIN

1. David McCullough, *John Adams* (New York: Touchstone, 2001), 285.

2. These words appear at the opening of Thomas Paine's pamphlet *The American Crisis*, published in 1776.

3. Rick Hampson, "Storms, earthquakes, North Korea and now the Las Vegas massacre: We have to wonder: 'What's Next?'," *USA Today*, October 3, 2017, https://www.usatoday.com/story/news/2017/10/03/storms-quakes-fires-korea-and-now-vegas-shooting-whats-next/725889001/.

4. Vance Havner, *Pepper n' Salt* (Grand Rapids: Baker, 1966), page number unknown.

5. Terry Wilcutt and Tom Whitmeyer, "Apollo 1-Challenger-Columbia Lessons Learned," *NASA*, https://sma.nasa.gov/docs/default-source/safety-messages/safetymessage-2014-01-27-apollo1 challengercolumbia-vits.pdf?sfvrsn=31af1ef8_6.

6. Andy Woods, "The Last Days Apostasy of the Church (Part 1)," *Bible Prophecy Blog*, November 19, 2009, http://www.bibleprophecyblog.com/2009/11/last-days-apostasy-of-church-part-1 .html.

7. John R.W. Stott, *The Message of 1 & 2 Thessalonians* (Downers Grove, IL: InterVarsity, 1991), 158 (emphasis in original).

8. Os Guinness, *Impossible People* (Downers Grove, IL: InterVarsity, 2016), 87.

9. John Phillips, *Exploring the Future: A Comprehensive Guide to Bible Prophecy* (Grand Rapids, MI: Kregel, 2003), 225, 269.

10. Ray Stedman, "The Deepening Darkness," *RayStedman.org*, December 21, 1975, https://www .raystedman.org/new-testament/romans/the-deepening-darkness.

11. Several variations of this story appear online.

12. "The Changing of the Guard," *Arlington National Cemetery*, https://www.arlingtoncemetery .mil/Explore/Changing-of-the-Guard.

## CHAPTER 11—SATAN'S SUBTLE SCHEME
## TO SILENCE BIBLE PROPHECY

1. Jeff Diamant, "About four-in-ten U.S. adults believe humanity is 'living in the end times,'" *Pew Research Center*, December 8, 2022, https://www.pewresearch.org/short-reads/2022/12/08/about-four-in-ten-u-s-adults-believe-humanity-is-living-in-the-end-times/.

2. "Biblical prophecy claims the rapture coming by month's end," *USA Today*, April 13, 2018, https://www.usatoday.com/videos/news/world/2018/04/13/biblical-prophecy-claims-rapture -coming-months-end/33762873/.

3. Kat Hopps, "End of the World: April 2018 Rapture prediction—will the world end?," *Express*, April 13, 2018, https://www.express.co.uk/news/weird/945306/end-of-the-world-april-2018 -rapture-prediction-will-world-end.

4. Tom Hughes is a former pastor and the founder of Hope for Our Times. His list appears in an article in my *Understanding the Times* newsletter, titled "The Pulpits Are Silent." You can

access the article at https://myemail.constantcontact.com/The-Pulpits-Are-Silent-.html?soid
=1101818841456&aid=xywCQABc3gI.

5. Amillennialism teaches there will be no literal millennial kingdom. Preterism holds that the prophetic events described in the book of Revelation were fulfilled in the first century AD. Kingdom Now theology says that Christians are to help God take back dominion of the earth, but God doesn't need our help to reclaim this world. Christ will do that at His return.

6. Rob Bell, "Rob Bell Tells it like it is," *Relevant Magazine*, January/February 2008).

7. Hank Hanegraaff, "Where Is the Rapture Taught in Scripture?," June 19, 2012, https://www.youtube.com/watch?v=eje2FjlAkVo.

8. For an overview of those who taught the rapture before John Nelson Darby, see Ed Hindson and Mark Hitchcock, *Can We Still Believe in the Rapture?* (Eugene, OR: Harvest House, 2017), chapter 5, "History of the Rapture Doctrine."

9. For a better understanding of what preterism teaches, see Thomas Ice, "The Trouble with Preterism," *Israel My Glory*, May/June 2009, https://israelmyglory.org/article/the-trouble-with-preterism/.

10. "Power," *US News & World Report*, https://www.usnews.com/news/best-countries/rankings/power (accessed May 6, 2024).

11. Paul N. Benware, *Understanding End Times Prophecy: A Comprehensive Approach* (Chicago, IL: Moody Press, 1995), Apple Books.

12. Maayan Jaffe-Hoffman, "Young Evangelical support for Israel plummets," *The Jerusalem Post*, updated February 12, 2024, https://www.jpost.com/christianworld/article-786545.

13. Jaffe-Hoffman, "Young Evangelical support for Israel plumments."

## CHAPTER 12—GOD'S PROPHETIC PULPIT IN THE LAST DAYS

1. A.W. Tozer, *The Pursuit of God* (Mansfield Centre, CT: Martino Publishing, 2009), 8-9.

## CHAPTER 13—THE TRIUMPHANT RETURN: WHEN JESUS COMES AS KING

1. Adapted from my commentary *Revelation: Unlocking the Future* (Chattanooga, TN: AMG Publishers, 2002), 187-197.

2. René Pache, *The Return of Jesus Christ* (Chicago: Moody, 1955), 353.

3. David Jeremiah, *The Book of Signs* (Nashville, TN: Thomas Nelson, 2019), 352.

4. Anthony Hoekema, *The Bible and the Future* (Grand Rapids, MI: Wm. B. Eerdmans, 1979), 223-238. Hoekema goes to great lengths attempting to prove that the marriage in chapter 20 precedes the return in chapter 19, which defies the clear logic of the sequence of events that are obvious in the text. Thus, he is forced to admit: "If, then, one thinks of Revelation 20 as setting forth what follows chronologically after what has been described in chapter 19, one would indeed conclude that the millennium of Revelation 20:1-6 will come after the return of Christ" (226).

5. Robert Gromacki, "Where Is 'the Church' in Revelation 4–19?" in Thomas Ice and Timothy Demy, eds., *When the Trumpet Sounds* (Eugene, OR: Harvest House, 1995), 335.

6. G.R. Beasley-Murray, *The Book of Revelation* (London: Marshall Morgan & Scott, 1978), 270.

7. Beasley-Murray, *The Book of Revelation*, 271.

8. Beasley-Murray, *The Book of Revelation*, 273-274.

9. Bruce Metzger, *Breaking the Code: Understanding the Book of Revelation* (Nashville, TN: Abingdon Press, 1995), 90.

10. Metzger, *Breaking the Code*, 90.

11. Robert Thomas, *Revelation 8–22* (Chicago: Moody, 1995), 381.

12. Warren Wiersbe, *Wiersbe's Expository Outlines on the New Testament* (Wheaton, IL: Victor Books, 1992), electronic edition.

13. A.W. Boehm, as cited in Johann Arndt, *True Christianity* (London: Brown & Downing, 1720), xxii.

To learn more about our Harvest Prophecy resources, please visit:

## www.HarvestProphecyHQ.com

**HARVEST PROPHECY**
An Imprint of Harvest House Publishers